OUR FOOD

THE KOSHER KITCHEN UPDATED

Anita Hirsch

Photography by Alison Miksch

Food and Prop Styling by Kay Lichthardt

DOUBLEDAY

New York London Toronto Sydney Auckland

A KENAN BOOK

PUBLISHED BY DOUBLEDAY

a division of Bantam Doubleday Dell Publishing Group, Inc.
666 Fifth Avenue, New York, New York 10103

DOUBLEDAY and the portrayal of an anchor with a dolphin are trademarks of Doubleday, a division of Bantam Doubleday Dell Publishing Group, Inc.

Library of Congress Cataloging-in-Publication Data

Hirsch, Anita, M.S.
    Our food : the kosher kitchen updated / Anita Hirsch ; photography
by Alison Miksch ; food and prop stylist Kay Lichthardt.
        p.   cm.
    ISBN 0-385-42215-6 : $25.00
    1. Cookery, Jewish.   I. Title.
    TX724.H57   1992   92-24948
    641.5'676--dc20   CIP

OUR FOOD
The Kosher Kitchen Updated
was prepared and produced by
Kenan Books, Inc.
15 West 26th Street
New York, New York 10010

Editor: Sharon Kalman
Art Director/Designer: Robert W. Kosturko
Photography Editor: Anne K. Price

Typeset by Classic Type Inc.
Color separations by Colourmatch Pte. Ltd.
Printed and bound in Singapore by Tien Wah Press

Dedication

I dedicate this book to Grandmom Rose Berman and all the Grandmom Roses
who came to America.

Acknowledgments

I want to thank everyone who made this book possible. Thanks to Dan Green for his faith and confidence; to Sharon Kalman for all her time and patience; and to Kay Lichthardt and Alison Miksch for the beautiful food photography. Thanks to my parents: my mom, Mildred Sher, who tasted and contributed her stories; my father, Morton Sher, who read and enjoyed what I wrote and always had time to edit. To my husband, Sy, who shopped with me and ate everything I made. To my children, Mike and Leanne, who helped me choose the best recipes and cheered me on. To my brother Marty and sister-in-law Carole Sher, who gave me ideas and encouraged me.

Thanks to my relatives who shared stories and recipes, especially Uncle Milton and Aunt Anita Berman, Uncle Mickey and Aunt Eleanor Schneider, Uncle Bernie and Aunt Doris Zod, Aunt Ann Glazier, and cousins Dick Berman, Rochelle Goldstein, Nancy Schneider, Robin Lerner, and Chuck Glazier.

Thanks also to my friends who tasted and gave their opinions: Susan Coraor, JoAnn Brader, Emily Folland, Marilee Stahler, and Janyn Bassett. Thanks to Rabbi Mitchell Raven, Director of Kosher Supervision for the Lehigh Valley Kashrut Commission. Thanks also to Yosi Horowitz of the Blue Star Wine Company in Philadelphia and to Matthew Green for their wine expertise.

INTRODUCTION

I was lucky...I was raised in a kosher home. By lucky, I mean that I did not really have to learn the kosher laws; I was brought up with them so they were easy to accept and adopt. I didn't know any other way. When friends ask me how I do it, how I avoid mixing meat and milk, how I keep two sets of dishes, I just shrug my shoulders because it's just the way it's done, like tying my shoes or brushing my teeth.

Keeping kosher makes planning meals a bit more thought-provoking; I have to think about each recipe a bit more, plan the meal, and be more creative with leftovers. Beans cooked in a meat pot can't be added to a cream soup. When buying food I have to read labels. I check ingredients for any dairy or meat products, and I look for a kosher symbol or the word "pareve." I want salad dressing to be pareve so that I can use it for dairy or meat meals. Because there is no need to check ingredient labels on fresh produce and grains, I use more fresh products.

Keeping kosher means the family has to think a bit more about the food and what's in it; they need to be more involved with meals. Not only do the kids ask "What's for dinner?" but they also ask "Is it meat or dairy?" They need to know the answer so they can set the table with the proper dishes and flatware. Actually, two sets of dishes and flatware make setting the table and the dining experience more interesting.

Mealtime is the focal point of the family—we always gather at this time and eat together. Thus the table is the center of the family: It's where to find out what's happening.

The focus of the Jewish holidays is discussing food and preparing the meal, and the foods served become an integral part of the tradition of the holiday. Last year my parents were in Florida during Passover, so my brother and our families carried on the tradition without them. My sister-in-law and I tried to prepare the same food in the same way our mothers

had. And my brother conducted the seders in the same manner as my father did.

My husband remembers that his family always ate Passover meals at his Grandmother Rose Hirsch's. There were no seders, and he can't remember the food served, but he does recall that the idea was to keep the family together. He reminisces about the Shupack family meals: "Every-

Above: The kitchen is often the focal point in the Jewish home. Here, Grandmom Rose, my mother, and my father clean up after a delicious meat meal. Opposite: There is nothing more traditionally Jewish than Matzoh Ball Soup (page 39). In my house it is served almost every holiday.

one would contribute something." The family met at Aunt Kathy and Uncle Phil's. Aunt Kathy made the brisket, challah, and rolls; Dora made the salad; Frieda made the kugels; and Ruth brought her pickles and the pies.

Following the kosher laws gives some boundaries to my life and the food I choose. Keeping kosher gives me some control over what I eat and when. Sometimes I even think the difficulty in getting kosher meat in Allentown is helpful in controlling my diet, especially because eating less meat, or less animal protein, is beneficial. It becomes a challenge to plan interesting, attractive, and healthful meals without meat.

In order for beef, lamb, goat, buffalo, deer, yak, chicken, turkey, duck, goose, dove, or pigeon to be considered kosher, it has to be killed by a "shochet," a religious person trained in ritual slaughtering. This licensed authority uses a very sharp knife that painlessly kills the animal. After an animal is ritually slaughtered, it is examined for physical conditions that could make it unclean or "trefah." If an animal is not killed in a ritual way, it is not kosher, and there is no way of making it kosher.

My mother tells the story of how her father selected a chicken to be slaughtered and put it into the old bathroom just outside the kitchen until he could take it to the shochet for the ritual slaughter. (For ten cents the shochet killed the chicken and for ten cents more, he removed the feathers.) Unfortunately, this particular chicken died somehow before it could be brought to the shochet and was given to gentile neighbors.

The last step in koshering meat is to remove the blood. I remember my grandmother and my mother bringing home meat and chicken from the butcher, soaking it for a half-hour, salting it for an hour, and rinsing it before using it. Now this soaking and salting process is done by the butcher. Kosher-packaged, fresh-frozen meats are always soaked and salted at the processing plant—information that is indicated on the package.

Fish does not have to be ritually slaughtered to be kosher, but it must have fins and scales. Gefilte fish is one of the three traditional Jewish foods—matzoh and cholent are the others. Because Jews cannot separate flesh from bone on the Shabbat, clever cooks decided to separate the fish from the bone prior to Friday evening and stuffed the fish skin with the chopped boned fish. Eventually the stuffing of the skin was forgotten. The tradition of preparing the gefilte fish has been declining because almost all gefilte fish is purchased in cans or jars, although many people still make their own fish for the holidays.

KOSHER COOKING: LOW FAT AND LOW CHOLESTEROL

If kosher means to you the heavy meals of Eastern Europe—beef roasts, potatoes, breads, and gravies—I want to dispel those thoughts. Kosher meals can be as delicious as they are low in fat and cholesterol. Some of the recipes I have included are popular favorites, modified by taking out much of the fat and salt. Brisket is here, but the fat is skimmed and discarded; the portions are

Above: I'm certain this scene is typical of nearly all Jewish gatherings—they always revolve around eating. Left: This Ground Turkey and Veggie Burger (page 86) is so delicious no one will know, or care, that it is made without beef. Opposite: The key to healthy eating is including lots of vegetables in your diet. This Orange, Carrot, and Onion Salad (page 55) is a delicious and exotic way of doing so—and it's pareve.

smaller, and it is served with high carbohydrate and low-fat kasha varnishkes. Salad dressings are made with less oil or no oil. Matzoh balls are made with egg whites and no salt. The chicken soup is made the night before so it can be refrigerated and the fat removed. (I remember my Mom skimming off the hardened fat and discarding it while my mother-in-law observed and finally remarked, "You are throwing away the best part!")

You'll also find that the traditional cream cheese and lox has been replaced with nonfat yogurt cheese and lox spread. Apple Streusel Coffee Cake isn't made with regular sour cream, but with nonfat sour cream, one egg, less butter, skim milk, and fewer nuts. Hamburgers are included, but they are made with vegetables and ground turkey instead. Lasagna is here but prepared with low-fat cheese, vegetables, and no salt.

Jews live all over the world and adopt the cuisine of the country in which they live. Since my heritage is a combination of Rumanian, Latvian, and Lithuanian, I prepare barley and bean soup, stuffed cabbage, pierogies, black bread, and kasha varnishkes. However, I also enjoy the cuisines of the Mideast and the countries bordering the Mediterranean Sea, so I have adapted all of these cuisines into everyday favorites. Because these recipes consist mainly of vegetables, particularly dried beans and grains, they are basically healthful. All these recipes are flavored with herbs and spices and use fresh, wholesome ingredients that can be quickly and easily prepared.

The microwave is a real time-saver, too. I also use a shortcut for making yeast breads: a quick-rising yeast that I combine with the flour rather than the water. This saves the step of waiting for the yeast to dissolve in the water.

Updated kosher cooking means cutting out some of the fat and cholesterol; serving lean beef and other red meats only three times a week; eating fish, turkey, or chicken; and using low-fat or nonfat dairy products, such as skim or 1 percent milk. I include foods that lower cholesterol: barley, oats, whole grains, skim milk, tuna, fish high in omega fatty acids, carrots, dried beans, soy beans, peas, garlic, and onions. I eat more vegetables, especially salads, and I use a variety of dark, leafy greens. I also stay away from hot dogs and cold cuts.

What my cousin Nancy remembers about Grandmom's kitchen is the dish of "gribenes" that was always on the stove. Grandmom would cut off the fat and chicken skin, add chopped onions, and cook the mixture until the fat liquefied and the onions browned. Then she poured that rendered fat into a jar. The browned skin and onions were placed in a dish for visiting grandchildren. We would fight over who got the gribenes on a piece of bread! Now I avoid eating chicken skin, and I cook with olive oil, canola oil, or polyunsaturated oil instead of chicken fat. Even these oils, however, should be used with discretion. Cut fat by using soft margarine as a spread, light mayonnaise as a substitute for regular mayonnaise, and fish packed in water rather than in oil. Also check labels for the amount and

type of fat in non-dairy substitutes. Fat-free mayonnaise and fat-free mayonnaise-type salad dressings are high in sodium, though, so observe the sodium content when you read labels. Use the low-sodium stewed tomatoes and low-sodium crushed and pureed tomato products, or purchase fresh tomatoes in season and freeze them.

Omitting eggs in recipes or substituting whites for egg yolks also helps to cut down fat and cholesterol. If a recipe has one or two eggs and serves six, it is not so important to substitute whites. Besides fat, there are beneficial nutrients in egg yolks such as vitimin K and B^{12}.

KEEPING A KOSHER KITCHEN

I do follow the kosher rules from the conservative tradition, and I have known kosher cooks who keep separate automatic dishwashers and separate sinks for milk and meat dishes. My mother kept separate bars of blue and white kosher soap and separate towels (red for meat, green for dairy) for each set of dishes. Now liquid detergents are kosher, and I usually don't dry my dishes.

Any dish that has been used for the preparation of both meat and milk, even if not at the same time (and thus has absorbed minute quantities of both meat and milk), is non-kosher. It is therefore necessary to maintain separate cooking and eating utensils for meat and dairy dishes. These must be properly marked or easily distinguished from one another by color, design, form, or size. Water glasses may be used for both dairy and meat meals.

A specified time period must elapse after one has eaten meat before one may eat a dairy product. There are different opinions as to the length of this waiting period. Acceptable practices range from a three-hour to a six-hour waiting period.

WHAT FOODS ARE KOSHER

In every community where there is an orthodox or conservative synagogue, there is a kashrut commission. The rabbi directs kosher supervision, attending all orthodox functions that utilize the kitchen (weddings, bar mitzvahs, etc.) and making sure that the ingredients of all foods to be used are kosher.

Kosher-packaged foods are usually identified by a symbol. A reliable symbol to look for is the U with the circle around it, the logo of the Union of Orthodox Jewish Congregations of America. Other symbols found on kosher products are noted in the appendix.

Above: This Passover Sponge Cake with Sliced Strawberries in White Zinfandel (page 113) is a pareve dessert, so it is the perfect end to any meal—milk or meat. Opposite: Sun-Dried Tomato and Bow-Tie Pasta Salad with Almonds (page 62) is a pareve entree, thereby eliminating any confusion as to which dishes to use and what to serve with it.

Pareve Foods

A food product containing neither meat, milk, nor their by-products is neutral. The Yiddish word "parev" (pareve) or the Hebrew word "stam" is used to describe this category. Pareve includes (1) everything that grows from the soil, such as vegetables, fruits, nuts, coffee, spices, sugar, and salt; (2) fish with fins and scales; and (3) eggs. Pareve foods may be eaten or cooked with either dairy or meat products.

A pareve food cooked in a meat vessel must be served in a meat dish and may not be eaten together with dairy.

Read the labels, especially the list of ingredients, to be sure that a product is kosher, and to determine if it is meat, dairy, or pareve. Food-labeling practices can be misleading: mono- and diglycerides or emulsifiers can be made from either vegetable or animal fats. Lactose may be manufactured from milk or molasses. The word "shortening" almost always indicates lard.

Some products that I particularly check for a kosher or pareve symbol are: pie shells, crackers, potato chips, pretzels; bread crumbs and breads; non-dairy creamers and margarines; hot chocolate mixes; powdered chicken soup mixes; baked beans; cheeses; mayonnaise and salad dressings; and cookies, cakes, pies, and puff pastries.

Contemporary Kosher

I do not look upon these kosher laws as restrictions of my diet; I have always thought that eating kosher was a healthier way to eat.

Dinner guests in my home can't tell by the menu that they are eating kosher food. Upscale restaurants around the country are offering seders serving Red Snapper Gefilte Fish, Roast Rack of Veal, Cumin and Eggplant Stew, and Honey Nut Cake. There are more than seventy kosher restaurants in Los Angeles and more than twenty thousand certified kosher foods.

Food from a kosher kitchen can be as delicious, cosmopolitan, and healthy as any cuisine. Kosher food can be included in the best of contemporary American cooking.

Gefilte Fish

Matzoh Meal Pancakes

Charoset

Chopped Liver

Potato Latkes

Tomato and Hot Pepper Sauce for Dips and Fish

Smoked Whitefish Salad

Stuffed Cabbage Rolls

Cheese Blintzes with Fresh Raspberry Sauce

Blintz Soufflé

Mushrooms Vinaigrette

Knishes

Yogurt Cheese Spread with Lox

Dorothy Hirsch's Chopped Pickled Herring

Antipasto di Mare

Kreplach

Sy's Pita Pizza

Hummus

Mike's Bruschetta

Roasted Eggplant Spread

CHAPTER I

APPETIZERS AND JEWISH HOLIDAY SPECIALTIES

GEFILTE FISH

PAREVE • MAKES 6 TO 8 BALLS

Traditionally eaten every Friday night, gefilte fish is now served mainly on holidays. In my grandmother's time, the preparation was an all-day project. She went to the fish markets to find just the proper combination of fish—she used equal amounts of "buffel" or buffalo fish, pike, carp, mullet, and whitefish—then she brought them home and kept them alive in the bathtub until she needed them. She skinned and boned the fish, ground it with vegetables, added matzoh meal and egg, and formed the mixture into balls. These were placed on top of the fish heads and bones in a large pot of water and cooked for several hours.

My recipe takes very little time since it is made with poached fillets. Leftover cooked fish is an excellent time-saver as well.

6   cups water
1   pound raw fish fillets: haddock,
        pike, carp, whitefish, buffalo
        fish, mullet, or a combination
2   carrots, peeled and sliced
1   stalk celery, sliced
2   small onions, 1 sliced and 1 finely
        chopped
2   egg whites, slightly beaten
1/4 cup matzoh meal
     Dash of pepper
1   teaspoon sugar
     Lettuce leaves
     Horseradish Sauce (recipe follows)
     Lemon slices (garnish)

Bring the water to a boil in a 4-quart pot. Turn heat to low, add the fish, and simmer for 5 minutes or until cooked through and white. Remove the fish from the pan and allow to cool in a bowl. Set aside. Reserve the cooking liquid. Add the carrots, celery, and sliced onion to the liquid. Mash the fish with a fork. Add the finely chopped onion, egg whites, and matzoh meal to the fish. (If a finer texture is desired, use a food processor fitted with a metal blade to combine ingredients.)

Wet your hands to keep the fish from sticking to them and form the fish into 6 to 8 balls. Bring the fish stock to a boil, lower heat to simmer, and add fish balls. After each ball is added, shake the pot slightly to keep balls from sticking together. Cover and cook for 1 hour. Almost all the water will be absorbed. During cooking, shake the pot occasionally and add water, if necessary.

Serve gefilte fish on lettuce with Horseradish Sauce. Chill if not serving immediately.

Per ball: 114 calories; 17 gms. protein; 9 gms. carbohydrates; 0.85 gm. fat; 68 mgs. cholesterol; 87 mgs. sodium

---

HORSERADISH SAUCE

PAREVE • MAKES 1/2 CUP

When I was in college, I had to prepare a lunch for a group of gentile friends. Since I knew they were unfamiliar with traditional Jewish foods, I decided to give them a sampling. Lunch began with gefilte fish and horseradish sauce. "Take a small piece of gefilte fish and dip it into the sauce," I said. They proceeded with apprehension. All put the food in their mouths at the same time and spit it out at the same time, squinting and crying. I thought it was the gefilte fish, but it was the horseradish sauce! I forgot to warn them that a little goes a long way.

1   4-inch chunk horseradish root
2   tablespoons apple cider vinegar
3   tablespoons red beet juice
        (optional)
1/2 teaspoon sugar
     Dash salt

Peel and cut the horseradish root into cubes. Place the cubes in a food processor fitted with the metal blade and process until grated. There will be about 1/2 cup grated horseradish. Add the remaining ingredients to the horseradish and process until smooth. Serve with Gefilte Fish.

Per tablespoon: 10 calories; 3 gms. protein; 3 gms. carbohydrates; 0 gms. fat; 0 mgs. cholesterol; 17 mgs. sodium

---

When Mom brought out the hand-turned meat grinder we knew it was gefilte fish time —and Passover. Gefilte fish, matzoh, and borscht with sour cream was a traditional Passover week lunch, served on green depression-glass plates and bowls—our Passover dairy dishes.

Passover at Grandmom Rose's; somehow there was always room for more. Even if you were seated at the far end of the dining table, you would still get plenty of food.

MATZOH MEAL PANCAKES
(Chremslach)

PAREVE • MAKES 12 TO 16 PANCAKES

I am including these because they are one of my husband's favorites. There are several foods that are traditionally served during the week of Passover, but not at the seder; this is one of those foods. I always serve the pancakes with confectioner's sugar sifted over the top. This recipe has been adapted from one in *Jewish Home Beautiful.* (Published by The National Woman's League of the United Synagogue of America, New York, 1958.)

3   eggs, separated, or egg substitutes
3/4 cup water
1/2 cup matzoh meal
1/2 teaspoon granulated sugar
    Dash of cinnamon
2   teaspoons confectioner's sugar

Beat the egg whites until stiff. In another bowl, combine the egg yolks, water, matzoh meal, granulated sugar, and cinnamon. Fold in the beaten egg whites. Heat a nonstick or lightly oiled iron skillet. Spoon about 2 tablespoons of batter into the skillet. When one side is golden, about 5 minutes, turn the pancake and cook the other side.
   To serve, place pancakes on a platter or individual plates and sift confectioner's sugar over them.

Per pancake: 42 calories; 2 gms. protein; 5 gms. carbohydrates; 1 gm. fat; 53 mgs. cholesterol; 16 mgs. sodium

CHAROSET
Chopped Apples, Dates or Raisins, and Walnuts

PAREVE • MAKES 2 CUPS

Charoset is one of the symbolic foods eaten at the Passover seder. Placed on the seder plate, its sweetness represents the hope of freedom. As part of the service, the bitter herbs are dipped into the charoset and then eaten. After that, the charoset is passed around to be eaten on or with matzoh.

1   large Red Delicious apple, cored, quartered, and peeled
1/2 cup finely chopped walnuts
1/4 cup chopped dates or golden raisins
2   tablespoons honey
2   tablespoons sweet Concord Grape wine
1/4 teaspoon cinnamon

Chop apple finely and place in a small bowl. Add remaining ingredients and combine well.

Per 1/4 cup: 96 calories; 1 gm. protein; 13 gms. carbohydrates; 5 gms. fat; 0 mgs. cholesterol; 2 mgs. sodium

Chopped Liver

MEAT • MAKES 2½ CUPS

This is a high-cholesterol food, but since it is eaten only occasionally, and it is traditional (and delicious), I am including it.

12   *ounces commercially frozen*
      chopped liver (see note)
4   *large hard-boiled eggs*
     Lettuce cups
     Sweet raw onion slices

Allow the liver to thaw in the refrigerator. Peel the eggs. Place liver and eggs in a food processor fitted with the metal blade. Process until smooth. Serve on lettuce cups garnished with thinly sliced onion rings. This can be used as a spread on crackers or thinly sliced rye or dark bread.

Note: To prepare chopped liver from scratch, use a pound of thinly sliced calves liver, or 8 chicken livers. In order to obey the kosher laws, the liver must be broiled so the blood runs out. Broil the liver 5 to 6 inches from heat for 5 minutes per side. Allow to cool. Sauté 1 large sliced onion in 4 tablespoons of corn oil until the onion is softened, about 15 minutes. Process the liver, onion, cooking oil, and 4 hard-boiled eggs as above in a food processor fitted with the metal blade. A meat or food chopper can be used. A blender will not make a satisfactory product.

Per ¼ cup (fresh or frozen chicken livers): 140 calories; 11 gms. protein; 3 gms. carbohydrates; 9 gms. fat; 284 mgs. cholesterol; 61 mgs. sodium

Potato Latkes

PAREVE IF SERVED WITHOUT SOUR
CREAM OR YOGURT • MAKES 16 LATKES

I always serve these as an entree at Hanukkah with a salad made of assorted fresh greens, broccoli, red and green peppers, and some shredded low-fat cheese. Latkes can be served as an appetizer at other times of the year, and they are especially nice when prepared in miniature.

5   *medium potatoes*
1   *small onion*
¼   *cup unbleached flour*
1   *egg or egg substitute, beaten*
¼   *teaspoon baking powder*
2   *tablespoons corn or peanut oil*
     Applesauce
     Light sour cream or plain yogurt

Shred the potatoes and onion with a hand grater or food processor. Add the flour, beaten egg, and baking powder. Add some oil to a large, heavy skillet and heat. Drop about ¼ cup of the potato mixture in a mound. Cook until golden brown and crispy on one side, about 5 minutes, and then turn, flatten, and brown the other side. Remove the finished latkes and place on a paper-towel-lined plate to drain any oil. Continue making the latkes, adding more oil only if necessary. Serve with applesauce and light sour cream or plain yogurt.

Per latke (estimated): 66 calories; 2 gms. protein; 10 gms. carbohydrates; 2 gms. fat; 13 mgs. cholesterol; 7 mgs. sodium

Every Hanukkah Pop and the grandchildren lit the candles. Once the candles were lit and the gelt was given out, everyone sat down to a dinner of Potato Latkes.

TOMATO AND HOT PEPPER SAUCE FOR DIPS AND FISH

PAREVE • MAKES 3 CUPS

This hot sauce makes a great appetizer when served with salt-free tortillas or taco chips. It is also delicious served with a plain broiled or baked fish. Drained and chopped canned tomatoes can be substituted for fresh tomatoes.

3 *jalapeño peppers, seeded and finely chopped*
1 *tablespoon cilantro, finely chopped*
12 *scallions, white and green part, sliced very thin*
3 *fresh tomatoes, chopped*
1/4 *cup olive oil*
1/4 *cup wine vinegar*

Combine all ingredients in a serving bowl. Serve with salt-free tortilla chips.

Per 1/4 cup: 48 calories; 0.4 gm. protein; 2 gms. carbohydrates; 5 gms. fat; 0 mgs. cholesterol; 3 mgs. sodium

SMOKED WHITEFISH SALAD

PAREVE IF PAREVE MAYONNAISE IS USED • MAKES 2½ CUPS

Smoked fish can be indulged in occasionally, and this fish salad is especially good at a dairy buffet.

1 *pound smoked whitefish*
2 *hard-boiled eggs*
1/4 *cup chopped onion*
1/4 *cup light mayonnaise (pareve)*

Skin and bone the whitefish. Mash the fish and the eggs with a fork. Add onion and mayonnaise and combine well. For a smoother consistency, process in a food processor fitted with the metal blade. Chill. Serve with whole grain crackers or pumpernickel bread.

Per 1/4 cup: 149 calories; 9 gms. protein; 1 gm. carbohydrates; 12 gms. fat; 74 mgs. cholesterol; 347 mgs. sodium

STUFFED CABBAGE ROLLS

MEAT • SERVES 12 (2 ROLLS EACH)

1 *large head of cabbage (3 pounds)*
4 *medium onions*
1½ *pounds lean ground chuck or turkey*
1/4 *cup plus 2 tablespoons uncooked converted or parboiled rice*
1 *(29-ounce) can no-salt added Italian tomatoes*
1/2 *cup brown sugar*
1/4 *cup apple cider vinegar*
1/4 *cup lemon juice*

Fill an 8-quart pot ¾ full with water. Bring to a boil. Cut out the cabbage heart with a vegetable corer. Place cabbage head in pot, turn off heat, cover, and set aside until the leaves are soft, approximately 30 minutes.

Preheat oven to 300° F.

Separate the cabbage leaves and spread them on a cotton towel. Grate one of the onions and combine it with the ground beef or turkey and the rice. Place a tablespoon (or less, depending on the leaf size) of the mixture in the center of each leaf of cabbage. Fold sides in and then roll leaves so that the meat mixture is secured inside. Do this until the rice mixture is used up. Slice the remaining cabbage and the remaining three onions and place in the bottom of a large, heavy pot. Place rolled cabbage leaves on top of the cabbage and onion. Pour tomatoes, brown sugar, vinegar, and lemon juice on top of the cabbage rolls. Cover and bake for 3 hours.

Per roll (using beef): 123 calories; 7 gms. protein; 14 gms. carbohydrates; 5 gms. fat; 19 mgs. cholesterol; 87 mgs. sodium

Per roll (using turkey): 91 calories; 8 gms. protein; 14 gms. carbohydrates; 1 gm. fat; 18 mgs. cholesterol; 87 mgs. sodium

Stuffed Cabbage Rolls can be served as an appetizer or as a main course. When the kids were young, they removed the cabbage and ate only the filling, so I often made unwrapped ones for them. Generally, I serve stuffed cabbage during Purim or Sukkot, but these rolls are delicious any day of the year.

CHEESE BLINTZES WITH FRESH RASPBERRY SAUCE

DAIRY • MAKES 12 BLINTZES

This makes a delicious dessert as well.

CREPES

3 · eggs or egg substitutes
1/4 cup skim milk
1/4 cup water
1/3 cup unbleached flour
Vegetable oil, as needed

Place eggs in a small bowl and beat well with a wire whisk. Add milk and water to the eggs and beat again. Slowly add the flour to the mixture, beating continuously as it is added until the mixture is smooth and thin. Heat a 7-inch, nonstick sauté pan on medium heat until hot. Add about a teaspoon of vegetable oil to the pan. Pour in 2 tablespoons of batter and tilt until the batter has covered the bottom of the pan. Heat until the batter begins to cook and the edges curl away from the sides of the pan. Invert the pan over a clean dish towel that has been spread out over a counter or table. The cooked crepe should fall easily out of the pan. When all the crepes are cooked, prepare the Cheese Filling.

CHEESE FILLING

MAKES ENOUGH FILLING
FOR 12 BLINTZES

My grandmother made this simple filling without eggs.

12 ounces dry curd low-fat cottage cheese or farmer's cheese
1 tablespoon sugar
Butter as needed

Pour off any liquid from the top of the cottage cheese and place in a small bowl. Add sugar and combine well.

To fill the blintzes, place a tablespoon of the cottage cheese filling in the center of the cooked side. Fold the two sides over the cottage cheese, turn the bottom up over the cheese, and then the top up and over, like an envelope. Fill all 12 crepes.

To complete the cooking, sauté the blintzes in approximately one tablespoon of butter until golden brown on all sides. Add more butter as needed. Serve with light sour cream, nonfat plain yogurt, applesauce, or Fresh Raspberry Sauce, and garnish as desired.

The blintzes can also be filled and served immediately, eliminating the sauté step and the extra butter. To serve cold (as in the photograph): take the crepe and turn it over so the cooked side is down. Then fill as above. Serve cold with the Fresh Raspberry Sauce and fresh raspberries.

Per serving (blintzes with filling):
94 calories; 8 gms. protein;
4 gms. carbohydrates; 5 gms. fat;
53 mgs. cholesterol; 19 mgs. sodium

FRESH RASPBERRY SAUCE

MAKES 2 CUPS

1 pint raspberries
2 tablespoons sugar (optional)

Mash raspberries in a food mill. Press the berry pulp and liquid through the mill to eliminate the seeds. Combine the berry puree and sugar to taste. Pour over cheese-filled blintzes or serve on the side.

Per serving (3 tablespoons): 10 calories;
0.2 gm. protein; 2.3 gms. carbohydrates;
0.1 gm. fat; 0 mgs. cholesterol;
0 mgs. sodium

I remember my grandmom Rose lining up in rows on a striped kitchen towel the crepes for cheese blintzes. She filled and served them with applesauce and sour cream. Cheese Blintzes with Fresh Raspberry Sauce is a great meal to make on Shavuos, when it is traditional to eat a dairy meal.

BLINTZ SOUFFLÉ

DAIRY • SERVES 12 TO 15 PEOPLE

4   *eggs or egg substitutes*
1   *pound farmer's cheese*
1   *pound part-skim milk*
     ricotta cheese
2   *tablespoons sugar*
2   *tablespoons lemon juice*
¹/₂ *cup skim milk*
3   *tablespoons corn oil*
¹/₂ *cup unbleached flour*
1¹/₂ *teaspoons baking powder*
     Fresh Raspberry Sauce (page 22)

Spray an 8- by 12-inch glass pan with non-stick cooking spray. Preheat oven to 350° F.

Beat 2 of the eggs in a large bowl and add the farmer's cheese, ricotta, sugar, and lemon juice. Mix well and spread over the bottom of the pan. In the same bowl, combine the remaining 2 eggs, skim milk, oil, flour, and baking powder and beat with a wire whisk until well combined. The mixture will be thin. Pour this over the cheese mixture already in the pan. Bake for 45 minutes until the top is golden brown. Remove from the oven and cool slightly. Cut into 12 to 15 squares. Serve with Fresh Raspberry Sauce, strawberries, blueberries, or nonfat plain or vanilla yogurt.

---

*Per serving (based on 12 servings):
207 calories; 13 gms. protein;
12 gms. carbohydrates; 12 gms. fat;
83 mgs. cholesterol; 74 mgs. sodium*

MUSHROOMS VINAIGRETTE

PAREVE • SERVES 6

Mushrooms are a low-calorie treat. These are lower in calories than the usual marinated mushrooms because only a tiny bit of oil is used. Drain and include on an antipasto plate or serve with toothpicks.

¹/₂ *pound small whole button*
     mushrooms
1   *scallion, white and green parts,*
     thinly sliced
2   *tablespoons lemon juice*
2   *tablespoons apple cider vinegar*
1   *tablespoon chopped parsley*
1   *tablespoon olive oil*
¹/₂ *teaspoon Italian seasoning*
     Freshly ground black pepper

Rinse and clean the mushrooms. Combine remaining ingredients in a serving bowl. Add mushrooms and coat all sides with marinade. Chill at least one hour before serving.

---

*Per serving (estimated): 32 calories;
0.9 gm. protein; 3 gms. carbohydrates;
2.4 gms. fat; 0 mgs. cholesterol;
1.5 mgs. sodium*

KNISHES

PAREVE WITH POTATO FILLING,
OTHERWISE MEAT • MAKES 24 KNISHES

This recipe is somewhat different because the filling is spread over a rolled dough, then the dough is hand rolled over the filling, sliced, and baked.

I made my first knishes when I was a young bride and wanted to impress my husband. I got the recipe from Jennie Grossinger's *The Art of Jewish Cooking*. I remember my first effort as being oily; but they had the right taste. I still have Jennie's book; it is a wonderful reference.

Here's my new version, with less fat and less cholesterol because it is made with ground turkey, onions browned in a little oil, egg whites, and rice. Barley, buckwheat, or any leftover cooked grain can be used instead of rice. I'll bet that's how knishes began: an inventive, frugal mother's way to use leftovers.

KNISH DOUGH

2¹/₂ *cups unbleached flour*
1   *teaspoon baking powder*
2   *eggs or egg substitutes*
¹/₄ *cup corn oil*
¹/₄ *cup water*

Preheat oven to 375° F.

Combine the flour and baking powder in a bowl. Make a well in the center and drop the eggs, oil, and water into it. Work the flour mixture by hand and knead until smooth.

Knishes can be formed two ways. One is to divide the dough into four parts and roll each as thin as possible into a rectangle

12 by 6 inches. Spread ¼ of the filling down the middle of each rectangle and roll up. Cut the roll into 1½-inch slices. Spray a baking sheet with nonstick spray, then place the rolled knishes on the baking sheet. Press down lightly to flatten. The second way to form them is to cut the rolled dough into 3-inch circles. Place a scant tablespoon of the filling on each; draw the edges together and pinch firmly. Place on a sprayed baking sheet, pinched edges up.

Either way you decide to form them, bake for 20 to 25 minutes or until lightly browned.

POTATO FILLING

MAKES 2 CUPS OF FILLING; ENOUGH FOR 24 KNISHES

1   cup chopped onion
2   tablespoons corn oil
2   cups mashed potatoes
2   egg whites
¼   teaspoon freshly ground
       black pepper

Brown the onions in the oil. Beat in the potatoes, egg whites, and pepper until fluffy. Fill knishes as described above.

Per potato knish: 108 calories; 3 gms. protein; 15 gms. carbohydrates; 4 gms. fat; 18 mgs. cholesterol; 11 mgs. sodium

GROUND TURKEY FILLING

MAKES 2 CUPS; ENOUGH TO FILL 24 KNISHES

½   cup chopped onion
1   tablespoon vegetable oil
½   pound ground turkey (any leftover
       cooked meat can be used)
½   cup cooked rice or buckwheat
1   egg white
       Dash of freshly ground
          black pepper

Lightly brown the onions in the oil. Add turkey and sauté until cooked. Add rice or buckwheat, egg white, and pepper, mixing together well. Fill knishes as described above.

Per turkey knish: 97 calories; 4 gms. protein; 11 gms. carbohydrates; 4 gms. fat; 24 mgs. cholesterol; 17 mgs. sodium

Here are Sy and I—the new bride and groom. Knishes filled with potato, beef, or kasha were among the traditional hors d'oeuvres passed to the guests. When we moved into our first home, I tried to prepare them myself—they weren't as good as at the wedding, perhaps, but a successful first try.

YOGURT CHEESE SPREAD WITH LOX

DAIRY • MAKES ⅔ CUP

Unlike cream cheese or light cream cheese, this spread is fat-free. Draining the yogurt overnight results in a nonfat, thick, spreadable product.

8   ounces plain nonfat yogurt
3   tablespoons shredded or chopped
      Nova Scotia salmon
2   teaspoons chopped fresh dill
2   teaspoons chopped onion

Line a colander or strainer with several layers of cheesecloth or a paper coffee filter. Pour the yogurt into the colander and place over a bowl. Allow to drain in the refrigerator overnight. The remaining ½ cup yogurt will be thick. Scrape the yogurt cheese into a small bowl and add the lox, dill, and onion. Serve chilled on bagels, miniature bagels, or whole grain crackers.

Per tablespoon: 17 calories; 2 gms. protein; 2 gms. carbohydrates; 0.2 gm. fat; 1 mg. cholesterol; 40 mgs. sodium

---

Toasted bagels and cream cheese are part of our traditional Sunday breakfast, as is probably true in many households. On special occasions we have lox, thinly sliced tomato, onion, and lettuce. Now we want to cut down on lox because of its salt and fat content, so I add some lox to nonfat yogurt cheese.

DOROTHY HIRSCH'S CHOPPED PICKLED HERRING

PAREVE • MAKES 4 CUPS

Pickled herring in cream sauce with onions is a traditional food for me. There was always a jar of Vita herring in the refrigerator when I was growing up. However, because of its high salt content, I now buy herring only on special occasions. When I buy it, I choose an assortment—pickled, creamed and chopped—and serve it with pumpernickel bread.

Herring is high in the healthy Omega oils—one of its advantages.

1   16-ounce jar commercial pickled
      herring, in wine sauce
1   carrot
2   hard-boiled eggs
1   Red Delicious apple, unpeeled,
      quartered, and cored
2   teaspoons lemon juice
2   teaspoons sugar

Drain herring. Put herring (including onions from the jar) and the remaining ingredients into a food processor fitted with the metal blade (Dorothy, my mother-in-law, originally used a meat grinder to chop the ingredients). Process until all ingredients are combined. Serve chilled with dark bread, bagels, or whole grain crackers.

Dorothy Hirsch, Sy's mother and the namesake for my pickled herring recipe.

ANTIPASTO DI MARE

PAREVE • SERVES 6

The fish highest in monounsaturated fats and Omega oils are herring, mackerel, sardines, tuna, and salmon. Norwegian sardines are especially good on an appetizer platter; they have a more pleasing texture and appearance than black-skinned, small Brisling sardines. Both can be used and both can be purchased packed in water. The Norwegian sardines packed in tomato or mustard sauce are a healthier choice than those packed in oil.

6.5   *ounces (1 can) red salmon*
3.75   *ounces (1 can) Norwegian*
        sardines in tomato sauce
6.5   *ounces (1 can) solid white tuna*
        in water
12   *leaves romaine lettuce*
1/2   *red onion, thinly sliced in circles*
1   *ripe tomato, cut into wedges*
12   *black olives (pitted or unpitted)*
1/4   *turnip, julienned*
6   *broccoli florets*
2   *tablespoons Fat-Free Vinaigrette*
        (page 56)
        Fresh herbs (garnish)

Drain the salmon, sardines, and tuna. Arrange the lettuce on a serving plate and arrange the fish on top. Place the remaining ingredients, except the dressing, decoratively on the plate. Pass the dressing on the side. Garnish with fresh herbs.

---

*Per serving (without dressing):
149 calories; 19 gms. protein;
5 gms. carbohydrates; 6 gms. fat;
37 mgs. cholesterol; 419 mgs. sodium*

KREPLACH

MEAT • MAKES 12 TO 16 KREPLACH

These stuffed dough pieces resemble wontons. Usually served in chicken soup, they are traditionally filled with ground meat. These are very much like Polish pierogies or the perogen of my Rumanian relatives. My grandmother drizzled molasses and honey over her kreplach. Mine are made with fresh ground turkey and I eliminate the chicken fat. I didn't change the egg in the dough since it is divided into so many servings. Kreplach can also be filled with mashed potatoes, ground liver, or any combination of these.

FILLING

1/4   *pound ground turkey or chicken*
2   *tablespoons finely chopped onion*
        Dash of finely ground fresh pepper
        Dash of cinnamon

DOUGH

1   *egg or egg substitute, beaten*
2/3   *cup flour*
1 to 2 *tablespoons water, if necessary*
6   *cups chicken stock or water*

To prepare the filling, combine the ground turkey or chicken with the onion, pepper, and cinnamon and set aside.

To prepare the dough, combine the beaten egg and the flour. Add water if necessary to hold dough together. Knead with oiled hands until elastic. Roll out on a lightly floured board until it is about 1/4-inch thick. Cut the dough into 2-inch squares. Place about 1 teaspoon filling in the center of the dough. Fold the dough into a triangle. Press the edges firmly together with the fingers. Placing a little water on the edges of the dough before sealing will help them stick together. Set the kreplach aside for 10 minutes. Bring the 6 cups chicken stock or water to a boil in a 3- to 4-quart pot. Drop the kreplach, one at a time, into the stock, lower the heat, and simmer for 20 to 30 minutes. Kreplach can be served in the stock as a soup, drained and served on a salad plate, or placed under the broiler until brown.

Per kreplach: 43 calories; 3 gms. protein; 5 gms. carbohydrates; 0.8 gm. fat; 24 mgs. cholesterol; 12 mgs. sodium

---

Antipasto di Mare is an easy beginning to a meal. Arrange the fish on a platter, surrounded by vegetables and fresh herbs. This dish is not only healthy but quick, and is a great addition to a dairy buffet or for break-the-fast after Yom Kippur.

SY'S PITA PIZZA

DAIRY • SERVES 6

This is my husband Sy's recipe. It's everyone's favorite.

6   pitas
1   cup canned no-salt added
       tomato puree
3/4 cup shredded part-skim mozzarella
       cheese
1   small onion, sliced
1/2 green pepper, seeded and julienned
6   large mushrooms, sliced
6   black olives, sliced
1   teaspoon oregano
1   tablespoon olive oil

Preheat oven to 400° F.

Place pitas on a baking sheet. Spread each with about 2 tablespoons tomato puree, then top with 2 tablespoons of the mozzarella cheese. Divide the onions, pepper, mushrooms, and black olives over the top of the 6 pitas. Sprinkle the oregano and drizzle the olive oil over them. Bake until the cheese has melted and the vegetables have softened, about 15 minutes.

---

*Per pizza: 193 calories; 9 gms. protein;
27 gms. carbohydrates; 6 gms. fat;
8 mgs. cholesterol; 309 mgs. sodium*

---

*Sy's famous Pita Pizza was a favorite at our
summertime food concession. It's quick and
easy to make, and each person can request
his or her favorite vegetable toppings.*

HUMMUS

PAREVE • MAKES 1½ CUPS

3/4 cup dried chick-peas (2 cups
       cooked) and 1/2 cup
       cooking liquid
3   teaspoons olive oil
2   tablespoons lemon juice
1   tablespoon tahini (available at
       Middle Eastern markets)
1   clove garlic, peeled and sliced
2   tablespoons chopped parsley
       (for garnish)
     Paprika (for garnish)

In a food processor fitted with the metal blade, add cooked chick-peas, 2 teaspoons olive oil, lemon juice, tahini, and garlic. (A blender can be used, but small amounts of the chick-peas have to be added to the liquid, which should be in the blender first.) Process until smooth, using the reserved liquid from the chick-peas; you will need at least 6 tablespoons. Spread the processed chick-peas on a flat plate or in a shallow soup bowl. Drizzle the remaining teaspoon of olive oil over the top. Spread parsley around the edge of the hummus and sprinkle the top with paprika. Serve with pita, pita triangles, or Pita Crisps (page 104).

---

*Per tablespoon: 30 calories; 1 gm.
protein; 4 gms. carbohydrates; 1 gm. fat;
0 mgs. cholesterol; 1 mg. sodium*

*Sy and I have spent the
summer with our families
"down the shore" in Atlantic
City since we were children.*

My son, Mike. His bruschetta is a favorite of anyone who eats it.

MIKE'S BRUSCHETTA

DAIRY • SERVES 6

My son, Mike, insists that this appetizer begin every party. It is easy to prepare and difficult to eat just one.

2	*tablespoons pine nuts, toasted (see note)*
1	*tomato, seeded and finely chopped*
2	*cloves garlic, peeled and minced*
2	*ounces shredded part-skim mozzarella cheese*
12	*thick slices French bread*
1	*tablespoon olive oil*
6	*basil leaves, finely sliced (for garnish)*

Combine the pine nuts, tomato, garlic, and mozzarella cheese. Place the French bread on a broiler pan. Brush the top side of each slice with olive oil. Broil the bread until golden, about 5 minutes, turn, and brush the other side with oil. Spread the tomato mixture over the bread slices. Place under the broiler and broil for several minutes, until the cheese melts. Remove from the broiler and garnish with sliced basil.

Note: To toast pine nuts, heat a small iron skillet. Add the pine nuts and heat on medium until they are golden on all sides. Shake the pan occasionally and remove nuts from pan when toasted (or they will continue to brown).

Per serving: 165 calories; 7 gms. protein; 20 gms. carbohydrates; 7 gms. fat; 5 mgs. cholesterol; 239 mgs. sodium

---

ROASTED EGGPLANT SPREAD (BABA GANOUJ)

PAREVE • MAKES 1½ CUPS

1	*medium eggplant (1 to 1½ pounds)*
2	*cloves garlic, peeled and sliced*
2	*tablespoons tahini (available at Middle Eastern markets)*
2 to 3	*tablespoons lemon juice*
⅛	*teaspoon cumin*
2	*tablespoons finely chopped fresh parsley (for garnish)*
6 to 8	*Greek olives (for garnish)*
1	*tomato, finely chopped (for garnish)*

Place the eggplant in the oven, under the broiler, or over a gas flame until the skin is seared and black, about 25 to 30 minutes. The flesh will feel soft and juicy. Cool for 10 minutes. Rub the skin off, holding the eggplant under cold water. Squeeze out as much juice as possible, since it is bitter. Using a fork, mortar and pestle, food processor, or blender, puree the eggplant. Add the garlic, tahini, lemon juice, and cumin and continue pureeing until well combined. Spread this mixture on a flat plate. Garnish with chopped parsley, olives, and tomatoes. Serve with pita, Pita Crisps (page 104), or other flat bread.

Per ¼ cup: 51 calories; 2 gms. protein; 9 gms. carbohydrates; 2 gms. fat; 0 mgs. cholesterol; 5 mgs. sodium

---

Baba ganouj is a delicious, low-fat way to prepare eggplant. Serve it in a hollowed-out eggplant that has been treated with lemon juice.

CHAPTER II

SOUPS

Today, making soup healthier means using less fat, less meat, and less salt. It also means including legumes, such as chick-peas, limas, and kidney or Michigan beans, to add fiber and to possibly lower your blood cholesterol. It means adding vegetables, such as cauliflower, broccoli, turnip, rutabaga, cabbage, bok choy, brussels sprouts, kale, and collard, mustard, and turnip greens to your soup, since they are the cruciferous vegetables that may prevent cancer and are high in vitamins and minerals.

It is fairly easy to create delicious soups that are low in fat. Eliminate cream and half-and-half, skim the fat off soups made with beef or chicken, and use less oil to sauté the vegetables. I always prepare the soup in advance so it has a chance to chill and I can remove the top layer of fat before serving. Using potato starch or yogurt instead of cream, sour cream, or half-and-half will thicken the soup just as well as high-fat ingredients. Pureeing one or two cups of soup in a blender or food processor will thicken the soup when it is returned to the pot.

One of the great things about soup is that it can be a meal in itself. It can be prepared while the cook is busy with other jobs, and by limiting the fat and sodium it makes a marvelous meal.

CHICKEN STOCK

MEAT • MAKES 8 CUPS

4	pounds uncooked chicken parts (preferably wings)
12	cups water
1	medium onion, cut in half (do not peel)
12	sprigs parsley
2	stalks celery, cut in thirds
4	carrots, scrubbed, cut in thirds
2	bay leaves
1/4	teaspoon black pepper

Place the chicken and water into a 6-quart pot or Dutch oven. Bring the water to a boil on high heat, then turn heat to low. Remove white foam with a slotted spoon. Add the onion, parsley, celery, carrots, bay leaf, and pepper. Cover the pot and continue to cook on low to medium heat. After one hour, turn off the heat and remove the bay leaf. Allow the broth to cool slightly, then strain the soup.

Remove skin from chicken. Take the chicken off the bones and cut it into chunks. Reserve it for another use. Remove the vegetables and reserve for another use, if desired. Refrigerate the stock overnight, then remove the fat that has formed on top and discard.

Per cup: 16 calories; 96 mgs. protein; 2.3 gms. carbohydrates; 0.72 gm. fat; 96 mgs. cholesterol; 24 mgs. sodium

Some things never change; at this Passover seder in 1948 my family was anxiously awaiting matzoh ball soup made from fresh chicken stock. Today, the players may have changed somewhat, but the anticipation remains.

CHICKEN NOODLE SOUP

MEAT • SERVES 6

If you have cooked cubed chicken, add a cup to this soup.

8   cups Chicken Stock (page 36)
1   carrot, peeled and sliced
8   ounces spaghetti, broken into 2- to 3-inch lengths
     Fresh dill, chopped (for garnish)

In a 2-quart pot, bring the stock and sliced carrot to a boil. Lower heat, cover, and simmer for 15 minutes, until carrot is tender. Cook spaghetti according to package directions and add to stock. Serve garnished with chopped dill.

---

*Per serving (estimated, without chicken):
168 calories; 5 gms. protein;
33 gms. carbohydrates; 2 gms. fat;
0.1 mg. cholesterol; 36 mgs. sodium*

HUNGARIAN SPLIT PEA SOUP

MEAT • SERVES 12

Split peas make a hearty soup. My mom always made hers with potato chunks and frankfurters. I serve hot dogs only occasionally because of all their fat, salt, and preservatives. This split pea soup is a little different because it has tomatoes, paprika, and caraway seeds to give it a Hungarian flavor. I like to make more soup than I need and freeze what's left over for another day.

1   tablespoon corn oil
1   green pepper, seeded and finely chopped
1   cup finely chopped onion
1   clove garlic, minced
1/4   pound lean chuck
1   pound dried split peas
1   cup canned no-salt added tomatoes
1   tablespoon paprika
1 1/2   teaspoons caraway seeds
3   quarts water
2   medium potatoes, peeled and cubed

Pour the oil into a 6-quart pot and heat at medium. Add the green pepper, onion, and garlic and sauté until softened, about 10 minutes. Add the chuck, split peas, tomatoes, paprika, caraway seeds, and water. Bring to a boil, reduce heat, cover, and simmer for 2 hours, or until split peas are tender. Add potatoes about 20 to 25 minutes before serving or they will become too soft and lose their texture. When soup is done, remove chuck, cut into bite-size pieces, and return to the soup. If you are freezing this soup, do so before adding the potatoes. Then, when you are reheating the soup, add cooked potatoes and some of their liquid to the soup.

---

*Per serving (estimated): 103 calories;
6 gms. protein; 16 gms. carbohydrates;
2 gms. fat; 5 mgs. cholesterol;
21 mgs. sodium*

Uncle Phil enjoys his favorite soup, probably barley and vegetable. Aunt Kathy prepared this soup for him every Shabbat.

MATZOH BALL SOUP

MEAT • SERVES 6

This recipe for matzoh balls uses only egg whites, not yolks. I served these to my family at Passover and they didn't notice the change; as usual, everyone wanted seconds.

4   egg whites
2   tablespoons corn oil
2   tablespoons water
1/3 cup matzoh meal
6   cups hot Chicken Stock (page 36)
    Chopped parsley (for garnish)
    Dash of black pepper (for garnish)

In a small bowl, beat egg whites with an electric mixer just until foamy. Combine with corn oil and water. Add matzoh meal and blend well. Cover bowl and refrigerate for 20 minutes. While the matzoh balls are chilling, fill a 4-quart pot with water and bring it to a boil. Reduce the heat slightly so the water remains at a low boil. Using your hands, form 6 balls of the matzoh meal mixture and drop them into the water. The balls will sink and then float. Cover the pot and cook for 30 minutes. When the balls are done, add them to the chicken stock. Garnish with chopped parsley and black pepper.

Per matzoh ball: 80 calories; 3 gms. protein; 6 gms. carbohydrates; 5 gms. fat; 0 mgs. cholesterol; 37 mgs. sodium

No Passover seder is complete without light, fluffy matzoh balls in a big bowl of home-made chicken soup.

CABBAGE AND TOMATO SOUP

MEAT • SERVES 6

This soup tastes better reheated. Instead of fresh cabbage, eight ounces of sauerkraut can be used, but this adds extra salt. Use lean, trimmed beef and there will be almost no fat to skim off.

1/2 pound lean chuck, cut into cubes
3   cups water
1   tablespoon canola or olive oil
1/2 cup chopped onion
1/2 cup chopped celery
1/2 cup chopped carrot
1   clove garlic, peeled and minced
1   pound cabbage, finely chopped
1   (16-ounce) can no-salt added
    stewed tomatoes
1   tablespoon lemon juice
2   tablespoons brown sugar
6   pitted prunes

Add meat and water to a 4-quart pot. Bring to a boil, then lower heat to simmer. Skim foam that forms with a slotted spoon. Heat oil in an 8- to 10-inch skillet; add onion, celery, carrot, and garlic. Sauté on low until vegetables are softened, 10 to 15 minutes. Add vegetables to the beef and water along with the cabbage, tomatoes, lemon juice, brown sugar, and prunes. Cover and continue to simmer for 2 hours.

Per serving (estimated): 170 calories; 10 gms. protein; 22 gms. carbohydrates; 6 gms. fat; 19 mgs. cholesterol; 71 mgs. sodium

CREAM OF BROCCOLI SOUP

PAREVE • SERVES 6 TO 8

1   bunch broccoli
2   tablespoons unsalted pareve
    margarine
1   medium onion, chopped
1   leek, sliced
1   carrot, peeled and sliced
2   cloves garlic, minced
4   cups water
4   teaspoons pareve powdered chicken
    soup mix
1   ripe tomato, chopped
2   tablespoons chopped parsley
4   ounces spinach, well washed
1/8 teaspoon nutmeg
    Dash of freshly ground pepper
2   tablespoons orange juice

Wash the broccoli and peel the stalks. Coarsely chop the stalks and florets. Add the margarine to a 4-quart pot on medium-low heat. When the margarine has melted, add onion, leek, carrot, and garlic. Sauté for 10 minutes until softened. Add the chopped broccoli, water, chicken powder, tomato, and parsley to the pot. Bring to a boil, lower the heat, cover, and simmer for 25 to 30 minutes. Add the spinach, nutmeg, pepper, and orange juice. Stir well and allow to cook, uncovered, for about 2 minutes. Transfer half the soup to a blender and puree. Pour into a clean pot and blend in remaining half. Stir well and serve.

Per serving (estimated): 108 calories; 5 gms. protein; 15 gms. carbohydrates; 5 gms. fat; 0 mgs. cholesterol; 146 mgs. sodium

RED BEET SOUP (BORSCHT)

PAREVE; DAIRY WITH SOUR CREAM OR
YOGURT • SERVES 6 TO 8

This is a pareve soup, until you add the sour cream or yogurt. Use light sour cream or nonfat plain yogurt.

    5   large beets
            (about 2 pounds total)
    4   cups water
    1   large onion, quartered
    2   bay leaves
    1/4 cup lemon juice
    2 to 4 tablespoons sugar
            Nonfat plain yogurt or light sour
            cream (for garnish)

Wash the beets thoroughly, cut off ends, and add to an 8-quart pot with the water. Bring the water to a boil, cover, lower the heat, and cook until the beets are tender, about 45 minutes. Remove the beets from the pot, saving the liquid. Measure the liquid and add enough water to make 6 cups. Peel and shred the beets, then put them back into the pot with the liquid. Add the onion, bay leaves, lemon juice, and 2 tablespoons of sugar to the pot. Cook on low for 20 minutes. Remove the onion and bay leaves. Taste and add more sugar, if needed. Chill. Serve with nonfat plain yogurt or light sour cream.

Per serving (estimated): 82 calories;
2 gms. protein; 20 gms. carbohydrates;
0.2 gm. fat; 0 mgs. cholesterol;
114 mgs. sodium

SPRING SORREL SOUP (SCHAV)

DAIRY • SERVES 6

This is a pareve soup until yogurt or sour cream is added. The egg thickens the soup, and although it adds fat and cholesterol, this one egg serves 6. Two egg whites could be substituted to cut the fat even more.

    1   pound sorrel (schav)
            (If sorrel is not available, add
            2 tablespoons of lemon juice to
            1 pound of spinach to achieve
            the sour flavor.)
    6   cups water
    1   cup chopped onion
    1   tablespoon vegetable oil
    1   egg or 2 egg whites
    1   tablespoon sugar
    1/2 cup nonfat plain yogurt or light
            sour cream (for garnish)
    1/2 cup finely chopped cucumber
            (for garnish)

Wash sorrel carefully. Separate stems from the leaves and chop each separately. Add the water to a 3- to 4-quart pot. Bring the water to a boil and add the chopped sorrel leaves. Cook for 20 minutes. Cook the chopped stems separately in a cup of water for 20 minutes until all the water is absorbed. Mash the sorrel stems through a sieve and put the sieved liquid and pulp into the pot of cooking leaves. The stems are too fibrous to eat, but the juices and pulp add color and flavor to the soup. Sauté the chopped onion in the oil until softened and then add to the leaves. When the leaves have finished cooking, beat the egg (or egg whites) in a small bowl. Add 1/4 cup of the hot cooking liquid to the beaten egg, whisking continuously. This prevents the egg from cooking too fast. Add another 1/2 cup of hot liquid, continually beating the egg mixture. Now add the egg mixture to the soup and beat well. Add the sugar and stir. Allow the soup to cool and then refrigerate until serving time.

To serve, spoon the cold soup into bowls and garnish with a dollop of nonfat plain yogurt or light sour cream and a tablespoon of chopped cucumber.

Per serving (estimated): 68 calories;
4 gms. protein; 6 gms. carbohydrates;
3 gms. fat; 36 mgs. cholesterol;
92 mgs. sodium

In our house, beet borscht is always served cold with a dollop of sour cream or yogurt.

CORN AND POTATO CHOWDER

DAIRY • SERVES 6

2 teaspoons canola oil
1/2 cup chopped onion
1/2 cup chopped red pepper
1/2 cup chopped celery
1 parsnip, peeled and cubed
2 medium potatoes, peeled
    and cubed
4 cups (20 ounces) frozen corn
1 bay leaf
1 cup water
1 1/2 cups 1 percent milk
2 tablespoons chopped parsley
1/2 teaspoon black pepper
1/2 tablespoon finely chopped red
    pepper (for garnish)
1/2 tablespoon finely chopped green
    pepper (for garnish)
    Plain nonfat yogurt (optional)

Heat oil in a 4-quart heavy pot. Add onion, red pepper, and celery and sauté until vegetables are softened, about 15 minutes. Add parsnip, potatoes, 2 cups of corn, the bay leaf, and water. Bring to a boil, lower heat, and simmer, covered, until potatoes are tender, 20 to 25 minutes. Meanwhile, puree the remaining 2 cups of corn in a blender or food processor. Add pureed corn, milk, parsley, and black pepper to the pot. Continue cooking until heated through, about 10 minutes. Remove the bay leaf and serve with garnish and a dollop of yogurt.

Per serving (estimated): 197 calories;
7 gms. protein; 42 gms. carbohydrates;
2 gms. fat; 3 mgs. cholesterol;
52 mgs. sodium

FISH AND VEGETABLE CHOWDER

DAIRY • SERVES 6

This main dish dairy soup is made with skim milk. The potato starch adds a creamy texture.

1 pound fillet of perch, cod,
    or haddock
3 cups water
1/2 cup orange juice
1 tablespoon corn oil
1 medium onion, peeled
    and chopped
1/4 cup chopped celery
1/4 cup chopped green pepper
1/4 cup chopped carrot
2 medium potatoes, peeled
    and cubed
1/2 cup no-salt added tomato sauce
1 1/2 tablespoons potato starch
2 cups skim milk
2 tablespoons chopped fresh parsley
1 tablespoon minced orange rind
    (optional)
    Freshly ground black pepper,
    to taste
1 tablespoon thinly sliced scallions
    (for garnish)
1 tablespoon finely chopped parsley
    (for garnish)

Add fish, water, and orange juice to a 6-quart pot. Bring to a boil and lower heat. Cover and simmer until the fish flakes easily, 10 to 15 minutes. Remove the fish to a plate; save the broth. In a 10-inch skillet, heat corn oil and add onion, celery, green pepper, and carrot. Sauté on medium-low heat until softened, about 10 minutes. Add the sautéed vegetables to the fish broth with the potatoes and tomato sauce. Bring the broth to a boil, lower heat to medium, and cook until potatoes are tender, about 20 to 25 minutes. Remove any bones from the fish and flake it into bite-size pieces. Add the potato starch to the milk and mix well. Add the milk mixture to the soup along with the flaked fish, parsley, orange rind, and black pepper. Continue heating and stirring until the soup is thickened and hot. Garnish each serving with scallions and parsley.

Per serving (estimated): 193 calories;
19 gms. protein; 21 gms. carbohydrates;
4 gms. fat; 33 mgs. cholesterol;
118 mgs. sodium

Growing up, we could always tell what day it was by the meal served at dinner. Thursday was a dairy meal, which usually began with a creamed soup, like this Corn and Potato Chowder.

BLACK BEAN SOUP WITH VEGETABLES AND RICE

MEAT OR PAREVE • SERVES 6 TO 8

This soup can be quickly done using stock made from one teaspoon of pareve chicken powder for every cup of water. Canned stock or homemade stock may be used as well. To lower the sodium in the recipe, cook dried beans without salt and use your own salt-free chicken stock.

- 1 cup dried black beans
  (4 cups cooked)
- 1 cup chopped onion
- 1 stalk celery, thinly sliced
- 2 carrots, peeled and sliced
- 2 cups Chicken Stock (page 36)
- 1/4 cup dry white wine
- 2 cups cooked converted or
  parboiled rice
  Dash hot pepper sauce
- 1 tomato, chopped (for garnish)
- 1 tablespoon chopped chives
  (for garnish)

To cook dried black beans, boil 1 quart water. Add raw beans, cover pot, and remove from heat. Soak 1 hour, then drain beans and return them to the pot. Add one quart of water to the beans, bring to a boil, cover, and cook on medium-high for one hour, or until tender.

Reserve 1 cup of the cooked black beans. Place the remaining beans and some cooking liquid in a blender or food processor fitted with the metal blade and puree. Add this puree to a pot with the onion, celery, carrots, Chicken Stock, and white wine. Cook until vegetables are tender, add the reserved beans, cooked rice, and hot pepper sauce. Continue cooking until the rice and beans are thoroughly heated, about 10 minutes. If the soup is too thick, add Chicken Stock. Garnish with tomatoes and chives.

Per serving: 256 calories; 12 gms. protein; 48 gms. carbohydrates; 1 gm. fat; .03 mg. cholesterol; 28 mgs. sodium

---

I started the tradition of serving Sweet Potato and Tomato Soup at Passover, but it is excellent for any family gathering. Of course, if you serve it at Passover, substitute matzoh for the crusty French bread.

SWEET POTATO AND TOMATO SOUP

PAREVE • SERVES 6 TO 8

This soup contains three vegetables high in beta carotene: carrots, sweet potatoes, and tomatoes.

- 1 tablespoon canola or corn oil
- 1 cup finely chopped onion
- 1 stalk celery, finely chopped
- 1 carrot, peeled and finely chopped
- 2 sweet potatoes, peeled and diced
- 1 (16-ounce) can no-salt added
  stewed tomatoes
- 2 cups water
- 1 teaspoon sugar
- 1/4 teaspoon nutmeg
  Chopped parsley (for garnish)

Heat the oil in a 4-quart pot on medium heat. Add the onion and celery. Sauté until celery is softened, about 10 to 15 minutes. Add the carrot and potatoes and sauté for 10 more minutes. Add the tomatoes and water and bring to a boil. Lower heat, cover, and cook until potatoes are tender, about 30 to 35 minutes. Remove two cups of the soup to a blender or a food processor fitted with the metal blade and puree until smooth. Return puree to the pot. Combine well. Add the sugar and nutmeg and continue cooking 5 minutes more. Garnish with chopped parsley, or as desired. Serve with crusty French Bread.

Per serving (estimated): 98 calories; 2 gms. protein; 19 gms. carbohydrates; 2 gms. fat; 0 mgs. cholesterol; 30 mgs. sodium

---

KALE AND WHITE BEAN SOUP

PAREVE • SERVES 6

3/4 cup dried white or Michigan
  beans (2 cups cooked)
3½ cups water
1 tablespoon olive oil
1 medium onion, peeled
  and chopped
2 cloves garlic, peeled and minced
1 stalk celery, finely chopped
1 carrot, peeled and finely chopped
1 bay leaf
4 cups water
8 ounces kale, washed and coarsely
  chopped, leaves only
1 tablespoon fresh dill
  Freshly ground black pepper
  (for garnish)

Soak the beans in enough boiling water to cover for one hour in a covered pot. Drain beans and add to a 3-quart pot with 3½ cups water. Bring to a boil, lower heat, cover, and continue cooking at a slow boil until beans are tender, about 1 hour.

Heat oil in a 4-quart pot. Sauté onion, garlic, celery, and carrot on low until softened, 10 to 15 minutes. Add bay leaf and 4 cups water and bring to a boil. Lower heat, cover, and cook for 20 minutes. Add drained, cooked beans, chopped kale, and dill. Cover and continue to cook for 10 minutes. Remove bay leaf. Serve garnished with black pepper.

*Per serving: 146 calories; 8 gms. protein;
24 gms. carbohydrates; 3 gms. fat;
0 mgs. cholesterol; 49 mgs. sodium*

LENTIL AND SPAGHETTI SOUP WITH TOMATOES, ONIONS, AND GARLIC

PAREVE • SERVES 6 TO 8

This is a vegetarian lentil soup; however, my husband enjoys it with hot dogs. So as a treat, I add (at the same time as the spaghetti) two hot dogs cut into ½-inch-wide rounds.

1 tablespoon olive oil
2 cloves garlic, peeled and minced
1 cup finely chopped onion
7 cups water
1 cup dried lentils
1 carrot, peeled and chopped
½ cup chopped celery
1 (14½-ounce) can sliced, stewed
  tomatoes (including juice)
  or 3 fresh tomatoes, peeled
  and cubed
4 ounces spaghetti, broken into
  2-inch lengths
2 tablespoons chopped parsley
  Dash of hot pepper sauce
¼ teaspoon freshly ground
  black pepper
½ cup dry white wine

Heat olive oil in a 4-quart pot. Sauté the garlic and onion on medium-low until softened, about 10 to 15 minutes. Add water, lentils, carrot, celery, and tomatoes. Bring to a boil. Turn heat to low and cover. Simmer for one hour. Add spaghetti, parsley, hot pepper sauce, black pepper, and wine (and hot dogs, if desired), and simmer until spaghetti is tender, 10 to 15 minutes.

*Per serving (without hot dogs,
estimated): 246 calories; 13 gms.
protein; 40 gms. carbohydrates; 3 gms.
fat; 0 mgs. cholesterol; 42 mgs. sodium*

To update the kosher kitchen, once full of fat and cholesterol, use more beans, leafy green vegetables, garlic, and onions. There's no better or easier way to do it than with a hearty soup, such as Kale and White Bean.

MIDEASTERN YELLOW SPLIT PEA SOUP WITH SPINACH AND CUMIN

PAREVE • SERVES 6 TO 8

1	tablespoon olive oil
2	cloves garlic, peeled and minced
1	stalk celery, chopped
1	cup chopped onion
1	carrot, peeled and sliced
1	cup dried yellow split peas
5	cups water
1	(14^1/$_2$-ounce) can no-salt added sliced, stewed tomatoes
^{1}/$_8$	teaspoon cayenne pepper
^{1}/$_4$	teaspoon freshly ground black pepper
1	teaspoon ground cumin Juice of 1 lemon
^{1}/$_4$	cup chopped parsley
5	ounces fresh spinach, washed and drained

Heat oil in a 6-quart pot. Add garlic, celery, onion, and carrots. Sauté for 10 minutes on low heat. Rinse the split peas and remove any impurities. Add to pot along with the water and bring to a boil. Lower the heat to medium-low, cover, and cook for 1 hour or until split peas are tender. Add tomatoes, cayenne, black pepper, cumin, lemon juice, parsley, and spinach. Cook for 15 more minutes.

Per serving (estimated): 103 calories;
5 gms. protein; 18 gms. carbohydrates;
3 gms. fat; 0 mgs. cholesterol;
51 mgs. sodium

TOMATO AND ORZO SOUP WITH GROUND BEEF

MEAT • SERVES 6 TO 8

This is a quick and easy soup. One or two cups of vegetables may be added; green beans, potatoes, and mushrooms are especially good. The soup improves with reheating. Add chicken or vegetable stock to thin out the soup if necessary.

1	tablespoon olive oil
^{1}/$_2$	cup finely chopped onion
^{1}/$_4$	pound lean ground chuck (If the chuck isn't lean, prepare the soup in advance so it can be chilled in order to remove the fat.)
4	cups chicken or vegetable soup (see note)
1	(14^1/$_2$-ounce) can no-salt added crushed tomatoes
1	cup orzo

Heat olive oil in a 6-quart soup pot. Add onion and ground chuck; sauté on low until onions are softened and beef is cooked. Add stock, tomatoes, and orzo. Bring to a boil, turn down to simmer, cover, and cook for 25 minutes or until orzo is tender.

Note: I make vegetable stock by saving the liquid from steamed or cooked vegetables. Then, I pour the liquid into plastic ice cube trays. When I need stock, I just pop out a few cubes and add them to soups.

Per serving (estimated, unskimmed):
168 calories; 7 gms. protein;
22 gms. carbohydrates; 6 gms. fat;
13 mgs. cholesterol; 41 mgs. sodium

LIMA BEAN, BARLEY, AND MUSHROOM SOUP

MEAT • SERVES 6 TO 8

1	cup dried lima beans
1	pound flank steak
2	quarts water
1	medium onion, sliced
8	ounces fresh mushrooms, sliced
8	ounces carrots, peeled and chopped
1	turnip, peeled and coarsely chopped
1	stalk celery, chopped
^{1}/$_4$	cup chopped fresh parsley
^{1}/$_4$	cup barley
2	tomatoes, peeled and cubed, or 1 (14^1/$_2$-ounce) can no-salt added stewed tomatoes
^{1}/$_4$	teaspoon pepper

Add lima beans to a large pot, cover them with water, and bring to a boil. Turn off heat, cover the pot, and allow the beans to soak for 1 hour. To an 8-quart pot, add the meat and the 2 quarts of water. Bring the water to a boil, turn heat down to simmer, and let the meat cook for one hour. After 1 hour, add the onion, mushrooms, carrots, turnip, celery, parsley, barley, tomatoes, pepper, and the drained, soaked lima beans. Continue cooking until the meat is tender and the vegetables are soft, about 45 to 60 minutes. Remove the meat from the soup, cut into bite-size cubes, and return to the soup.

Per serving (estimated): 258 calories;
21 gms. protein; 28 gms. carbohydrates;
8 gms. fat; 38 mgs. cholesterol;
110 mgs. sodium

TONY GOLDBERG'S "END OF THE WEEK" VEGETARIAN MINESTRONE

DAIRY • SERVES 6 TO 8

Tony Goldberg, a friend of my daughter, makes this soup with leftover vegetables. This is a meal in itself; everyone takes a big bowl and maybe even seconds.

³/₄ cup dried chick-peas
       (2 cups cooked)
³/₄ cup dried cannellini or kidney
       beans (2 cups cooked)
7   cups water
1   tablespoon corn or canola oil
¹/₂ cup chopped celery
¹/₂ cup chopped carrot
¹/₂ cup chopped onion
¹/₂ cup chopped green pepper
1   garlic clove, peeled and minced
2   (14¹/₂-ounce) cans no-salt added,
       sliced, stewed tomatoes
1   cup peeled and cubed potato
4   cups water
4   teaspoons pareve powdered
       chicken or vegetable soup mix
       (optional)
1   cup dry pasta (fusilli, rotini,
       or elbows)
1   teaspoon chervil
1   bay leaf
2   tablespoons chopped fresh
       parsley, including stems
1   teaspoon Italian seasoning
¹/₂ teaspoon oregano
¹/₂ teaspoon black pepper
2   cups leftover vegetables (peas,
       green beans, corn)
¹/₂ cup Parmesan or Romano cheese

Pour enough boiling water to cover chick-peas and cannellini beans. Cover and soak, off the heat, for one hour. Drain and add beans to a 4- to 6-quart pot with 3¹/₂ cups water. Bring to a boil, lower heat, cover, and continue cooking at a slow boil until beans are tender, about 1 hour.

Heat oil in a 6-quart pot. Add celery, carrot, onion, green pepper, and garlic. Sauté for 10 minutes. Add the stewed tomatoes and the potato and cook 10 minutes. Add the 4 cups water, powdered soup mix, pasta, drained beans, the herbs and spices, and cook for 30 minutes. Add leftover vegetables and the cheese and heat another 10 minutes. (The cheeses can be omitted for a pareve soup, or it can be used as a garnish for each bowl; about 1 tablespoon per serving. Lowering the cheese content will also cut down on the sodium.)

Per 2 cup serving: 462 calories; 22 gms. protein; 80 gms. carbohydrates; 7 gms. fat; 7 mgs. cholesterol; 250 mgs. sodium

Any vegetables are delicious in Tony Goldberg's Vegetarian Minestrone. A few suggestions include carrots, peppers, tomatoes, or radishes—go through your refrigerator and add whatever you have on hand.

Deluxe Pickled Cabbage

Bulgur Salad with Parsley and Pine Nuts

Corn and Barley Salad

Buckwheat Salad with Cucumbers and Watercress

Chunky Garden Salad

Orange, Carrot, and Onion Salad

Rice Salad with Tomatoes, Artichoke Hearts, Olives, and Golden Raisins

Jicama and Green Bean Salad

Little Caesar Salad

Couscous Salad with Red Lentils and Currants

Mom's Cole Slaw

Mom's Potato Salad

Leanne's Romaine, Pepper, and Sun-Dried Tomato Salad

Sun-Dried Tomato and Bow-Tie Pasta Salad with Almonds

Easy Pickled Beets

Cucumber and Onion Salad in Yogurt Dill Dressing

CHAPTER III

SALADS

When I thought about what traditional kosher salads to include in this cookbook, at first only cole slaw, potato salad, and pickled cabbage came to mind. But salads are where inventiveness and health run together. Since buckwheat served as kasha was traditional in my household, and since whole grains should be used more in our diet, I have included a buckwheat salad.

You should have a salad at least once a day. It doesn't have to be a recipe—just put together three or four raw foods as an accompaniment or as the main course. When you go shopping, pick one seasonal vegetable, one salad green (preferably not plain iceberg lettuce), a root vegetable such as carrots, and combine perhaps with a finely sliced scallion. I also like to add raisins, sesame seeds, and canned beans.

DELUXE PICKLED CABBAGE

PAREVE • MAKES 4 PINTS

1	small head (2 pounds) cabbage
1	sweet red pepper
2	Kirby cucumbers (each 5 inches long)
$\frac{1}{2}$	cup kosher or non-iodized table salt
$4\frac{1}{2}$	cups white vinegar
3	cups sugar

Wash, chop, and combine vegetables with salt. Cover with hot tap water and let stand 12 hours. Drain. Rinse with fresh water to remove salt. Pat dry with a clean white cloth or paper towels to remove as much liquid as possible. Combine vinegar and sugar in a saucepan large enough to hold all the vegetables. Heat to a boil. Add the vegetables and boil gently 30 minutes, or until the volume of the mixture is reduced by half.

Fill sterile canning jars with the hot mixture, leaving $\frac{1}{2}$-inch headspace. Put lids and screw rings on jars. Process by placing jars in a large pot of hot water. Make sure the water is 1 inch over the jar tops. Bring the water to a boil, cover, and boil for 5 minutes. Remove jars from pot immediately. Jars can be stored unrefrigerated unless opened. Without processing, jars must be refrigerated and will keep 3 to 4 weeks.

Per $\frac{1}{2}$ cup (estimated): 88 calories; 0.8 gm. protein; 24 gms. carbohydrates; 0.1 gm. fat; 0 mgs. cholesterol; 11 mgs. sodium

---

BUILD A SALAD

Use one item from each column or at least four or five different items for each salad.

VEGETABLES	NUTS/SEEDS/FRUITS	BASIC GREENS	OTHER
Artichoke hearts	Almonds, slivered	Arugula	Anchovies
Asparagus	Avocado	Chard	Cheese, Feta
Beans, cooked and dried	Berries	Dandelion greens	Cheese, shredded
Beets, plain or pickled	Canteloupe	Endive	Chicken
Broccoli	Cashews, unsalted	Mustard greens	Croutons
Brussels sprouts, steamed	Dates, chopped	Radicchio	Currants
Carrot	Grape Nuts cereal	Romaine	Egg whites, hard boiled
Cauliflower	Kiwi	Spinach	Roast beef, cold
Celery	Orange	Turnip greens	Salmon
Celery root	Orange rind		Tuna
Cucumber	Peanuts, unsalted		Turkey
Corn	Pecans, chopped		
Fennel	Raisins		
Green Beans	Sesame seeds		
Jicama	Sunflower Seeds		
Kohlrabi			
Mint			
Mushrooms			
Olives			
Onion			
Parsley			
Peas, raw or cooked			
Peppers			
Radishes			
Rutabaga			
Sprouts			
Tomato			
Turnip			
Watercress			
Zucchini			

BULGUR SALAD WITH PARSLEY AND PINE NUTS

PAREVE • SERVES 6

In the Middle East this salad is known as *tabbouleh*. The main ingredient, bulgur or cracked wheat, is enhanced by the parsley, mint, and lemon. I keep the oil to a minimum and add pine nuts, which can be omitted or cut down to lower the fat content.

1   cup bulgur wheat
2   cups boiling water
3/4   cup chopped parsley
1   large tomato, chopped
2 to 3   scallions, white and green parts, finely sliced
1/4   cup pine nuts
3   tablespoons lemon juice
2   tablespoons olive oil
1   clove garlic, peeled and minced
12   pitted black olives, sliced
2   tablespoons chopped fresh mint
      Cucumber slices (for garnish)
      Parsley sprigs (for garnish)

Place the bulgur in a medium-size bowl. Add boiling water and soak for 45 minutes. Drain the bulgur in a colander, pressing most of the moisture out by hand or with a wooden spoon. Add the drained bulgur to a bowl with all the other ingredients. Stir to combine.

Per serving: 173 calories; 5 gms. protein; 21 gms. carbohydrates; 9.6 gms. fat; 0 mgs. cholesterol; 50 mgs. sodium

CORN AND BARLEY SALAD

PAREVE • SERVES 6

Since this salad contains a complete protein combination, it is an excellent vegetarian main dish.

6   cups water
1   cup uncooked barley
1   10-ounce package frozen corn, thawed, or 1 (11-ounce) can low-sodium corn
6   scallions, white and green parts, thinly sliced
1   tomato, chopped
1   jalapeño pepper, seeded and finely chopped
3   tablespoons white wine vinegar
3   tablespoons olive oil
1/2   teaspoon cumin
3   tablespoons minced fresh cilantro

Bring the water to a boil in a large saucepan. Add the barley, lower the heat, cover, and cook for 45 minutes, until barley is just tender. I prefer regular barley, but instant barley can be used. Drain in a colander. Cool. Place barley in a large serving bowl. Add the corn, scallions, tomato, and jalapeño pepper and toss. Drizzle the vinegar and oil over the salad and sprinkle on the cumin. Mix the salad and dressing with a spoon until well combined. Add cilantro just before serving and combine well.

Per serving: 223 calories; 5 gms. protein; 38 gms. carbohydrates; 7 gms. fat; 0 mgs. cholesterol; 9 mgs. sodium

BUCKWHEAT SALAD WITH CUCUMBERS AND WATERCRESS

PAREVE • SERVES 6

The longer this salad marinates, the better it tastes.

1   cup buckwheat groats
1   egg white
1 3/4   cups water
3   scallions, minced
1   cucumber, peeled and finely chopped
2   cups watercress
3   tablespoons lemon juice
3   tablespoons canola oil
1/4   cup chopped, pitted dates

Combine buckwheat and egg white in a bowl. Stir with a fork until all the groats are coated. Heat a heavy or Teflon-coated saucepan. When hot, add the groats and cook and stir until the grains are dry and separate. Add the water and bring to a boil. Lower heat, cover, and cook for 10 minutes. Spoon the cooked buckwheat into a serving bowl. Add the remaining ingredients. Mix well. Chill until serving time.

Per serving: 191 calories; 5 gms. protein; 28 gms. carbohydrates; 8 gms. fat; 0 mgs. cholesterol; 15 mgs. sodium

CHUNKY GARDEN SALAD

PAREVE • SERVES 6

This is my favorite salad. The black and green olives and the artichoke hearts make it special. There is never any left.

1   pint cherry tomatoes
1   (16-ounce) can artichoke hearts, drained, or 1 (10-ounce) package frozen hearts, thawed
1   cup pitted black olives, drained
1   cup pimiento-stuffed green olives, drained
1   large cucumber, peeled and sliced
1   carrot, peeled and sliced
1   cup raw cauliflower florets
6   red onion slices
4   ounces raw mushrooms, sliced
1   teaspoon prepared mustard
1/3 cup red wine vinegar
2   tablespoons corn oil
1   tablespoon olive oil
1/4 teaspoon black pepper

Combine the vegetables in a salad bowl. Whisk together the mustard, vinegar, oils, and pepper. Pour over the salad. Combine well and serve.

Per serving: 133 calories; 4 gms. protein; 13 gms. carbohydrates; 10 gms. fat; 0 mgs. cholesterol; 250 mgs. sodium

Orange, Carrot, and Onion Salad reminds me of Israel. It is a delicious and different salad to serve at the seder.

Using different kinds of lettuce adds variety and color to a salad.

ORANGE, CARROT, AND ONION SALAD

PAREVE • SERVES 6

1   pound carrots
2   cups water
1   small red onion, peeled and sliced
1/2 cup orange juice
1   tablespoon sugar
2   tablespoons apple cider vinegar
2   tablespoons canola or olive oil
1   teaspoon dry mustard
1/8 teaspoon black pepper
12 cups torn salad greens or leaf lettuce

Wash, peel, and slice carrots into 1/4-inch-thick rounds, or shred them. Bring 2 cups of water to a boil in a saucepan. Add carrots, cover, and cook on medium-high heat for 8 minutes, until tender. If shredding carrots, cook 3 to 4 minutes. Drain. Transfer carrots to a bowl with the sliced onion. Add remaining ingredients, except greens, to the bowl. Toss well to combine. Marinate for several hours or overnight. Serve over salad greens.

Per serving: 105 calories; 2 gms. protein; 15 gms. carbohydrates; 5 gms. fat; 0 mgs. cholesterol; 35 mgs. sodium

RICE SALAD WITH TOMATOES, ARTICHOKE HEARTS, OLIVES, AND GOLDEN RAISINS

PAREVE • SERVES 6

Brown rice is more nutritious than white rice. If you don't like it, you might try a combination of the two. If not, use white rice that has been converted or parboiled.

3	cups water
1¹/₂	cups uncooked rice
¹/₂	cup golden raisins
1	sweet red pepper, seeded and thinly sliced
1	(16-ounce) can artichoke hearts, drained
1	tomato, chopped
6	pitted black olives, quartered
1	cup fresh peas (sugar snap or regular)
¹/₃	cup Fat-Free Vinaigrette or Low-Fat Ranch dressing (recipes follow)

Bring 3 cups of water to a boil. Add rice, cover, and lower heat. Cook brown rice for 20 to 30 minutes and white rice 10 to 15 minutes, following directions on the box. When rice is cooked, pour into a colander and cool. Set aside. Put raisins in a bowl of hot water and soak for 10 minutes. Drain. Place the cooled rice in a bowl. Add remaining ingredients, including raisins, and combine well.

Per serving (without dressing): 188 calories; 6 gms. protein; 40 gms. carbohydrates; 2 gms. fat; 0 mgs. cholesterol; 55 mgs. sodium

---

LOW-FAT RANCH DRESSING

DAIRY • MAKES 1 CUP

³/₄	cup nonfat plain yogurt
¹/₄	cup light or fat-free mayonnaise
2	tablespoons tarragon vinegar
1	tablespoon minced onion
2	teaspoons minced parsley
¹/₈	teaspoon celery seed
¹/₂	teaspoon Dijon mustard
¹/₈	teaspoon garlic powder

Combine ingredients well. Chill before serving.

Per 2-tablespoon serving: 33 calories; 1 gm. protein; 3 gms. carbohydrates; 2 gms. fat; 0.4 mg. cholesterol; 61 mgs. sodium

---

FAT-FREE VINAIGRETTE

PAREVE • MAKES 1 CUP

¹/₃	cup lemon juice
¹/₃	cup white wine vinegar
¹/₃	cup frozen apple juice concentrate
2	teaspoons Dijon mustard
1	teaspoon dried basil
1	teaspoon dried oregano
	Freshly ground pepper

Combine all ingredients in a jar. Cover and shake to mix.

Per 2-tablespoon serving: 24 calories; 2 gms. protein; 7 gms. carbohydrates; 0.1 gm. fat; 0 mgs. cholesterol; 20 mgs. sodium

---

JICAMA AND GREEN BEAN SALAD

PAREVE • SERVES 6

2	cups frozen French-cut green beans
1	cup jicama, julienned
2	roasted red peppers (see page 70), cut into thin strips
10	pitted black olives, quartered
2	tablespoons lemon juice
¹/₈	teaspoon finely chopped lemon zest
1	tablespoon olive oil
	Freshly ground black pepper, to taste

Cook beans in boiling water for 4 minutes. Drain. Place in a serving bowl and add the jicama, roasted red peppers, and black olives. Combine remaining ingredients. Pour over salad and toss.

Per serving: 56 calories; 1 gm. protein; 6 gms. carbohydrates; 4 gms. fat; 0 mgs. cholesterol; 40 mgs. sodium

---

LITTLE CAESAR SALAD

DAIRY • SERVES 6

Caesar salad is usually made with romaine lettuce, oil-drenched croutons, raw eggs, olive oil, and Parmesan cheese. This version uses egg substitute, not only to lower cholesterol, but to ensure a salmonella-free product.

1 head romaine lettuce
2 cloves garlic, peeled and minced
1/4 cup egg substitute
1/2 cup Low-Fat Vinaigrette
      (recipe follows)
1 cup croutons (see note)
4 anchovy filets, chopped (optional)
1 tablespoon grated Parmesan cheese
      (optional)

Separate and wash the lettuce leaves and spin or pat dry. Whisk together the garlic and egg substitute in a large salad bowl. Add the Low-Fat Vinaigrette and whisk again. Tear the romaine leaves into the bowl. Toss with the dressing. Add the croutons, anchovies, and cheese. Toss and serve immediately.

Note: To prepare the croutons, cube 2 slices of whole grain bread and bake at 350°F for 20 minutes, turning to brown all sides.

Per serving (using all dressing):
69 calories; 5 gms. protein;
9 gms. carbohydrates; 2.2 gms. fat;
3 mgs. cholesterol; 209 mgs. sodium

LOW-FAT VINAIGRETTE

PAREVE • MAKES 1 CUP

2 cloves garlic, peeled and minced
2 teaspoons Italian seasoning
1 tablespoon Dijon or Parisienne-
      style mustard
1 tablespoon olive oil
6 tablespoons balsamic vinegar
1/2 cup apple juice or white grape juice

Combine all ingredients in a jar. Close top and shake to mix.

Per 2-tablespoon serving: 26 calories;
0.1 gm. protein; 3 gms. carbohydrates;
2 gms. fat; 0 mgs. cholesterol;
25 mgs. sodium

My daughter, Leanne (as a child, above), loves Caesar salad. My version is relatively healthy because it is made with egg equivalents and uses a low-fat vinaigrette.

COUSCOUS SALAD WITH RED LENTILS AND CURRANTS

MEAT • SERVES 6

This can also be served cold over unusual greens such as curly endive or frisée.

2 cups chicken stock (pareve powdered chicken soup mix may be used)
1/2 cup dried red or yellow lentils
1 cup couscous
1/4 cup currants
2 scallions, finely sliced
2 tablespoons olive oil
1 tablespoon lemon juice
   Minced scallions, white and green parts (for garnish)

Bring chicken stock to a boil. Add red lentils, lower heat, cover, and cook for 5 minutes or until tender. If using yellow lentils, cook for 15 minutes, or until tender. Add couscous and currants; stir until combined. Remove from heat and let stand for 5 minutes. Transfer to a bowl and stir to fluff. Add scallions, olive oil, and lemon juice. Garnish with minced scallions.

Per serving: 234 calories;
9 gms. protein; 38 gms. carbohydrates;
5 gms. fat; 0.03 mg. cholesterol;
10 mgs. sodium

Couscous is a staple of Mediterranean and Middle Eastern Cuisines. The addition of red lentils and currants gives it an exotic taste.

MOM'S COLE SLAW

PAREVE • SERVES 6

My mom makes the best pareve cole slaw; she usually makes four times this recipe for family gatherings. I use a light or fat-free mayonnaise.

6 cups shredded cabbage
1 carrot, peeled and shredded
4 radishes, thinly sliced
1 tablespoon sugar
1 tablespoon apple cider vinegar
3 tablespoons light mayonnaise (pareve)
3 tablespoons unflavored seltzer or water
1/4 teaspoon black pepper

Combine all ingredients in a serving bowl. Marinate at least one hour before serving.

Per serving: 55 calories; 1 gm. protein;
9 gms. carbohydrates; 2 gms. fat;
0 mgs. cholesterol; 61 mgs. sodium

My mother taught me everything she knows about cole slaw. The only difference between hers and mine is that I cut down on fat and cholesterol by using light or fat-free mayonnaise.

MOM'S POTATO SALAD

PAREVE • SERVES 6

This is my version of the potato salad Mom always made. Mine is made a bit healthier by leaving out added salt, cutting down on the mayonnaise, and, of course, using a light mayonnaise to decrease the fat.

3   *large Idaho potatoes, peeled and cubed*
2   *teaspoons sugar*
2   *teaspoons distilled white vinegar*
1/2 *cup chopped onion*
1/2 *cup chopped celery*
1/4 *cup chopped parsley*
1 1/2 *teaspoons celery seed*
1/2 *cup light mayonnaise (pareve)*

Add potatoes to a 4-quart pot, cover with water, and bring to a boil. Reduce heat to medium, cover, and cook until tender, about 10 minutes. Drain potatoes. Place them in a large bowl and sprinkle with sugar and vinegar. Add remaining ingredients. Mix well so that all potatoes are coated with dressing. Chill.

Per serving: 173 calories; 3 gms. protein;
29 gms. carbohydrates; 6 gms. fat;
0 mgs. cholesterol; 124 mgs. sodium

LEANNE'S ROMAINE, PEPPER, AND SUN-DRIED TOMATO SALAD

DAIRY • SERVES 6

This is a wonderful salad that my daughter Leanne invented. I love watching her taste and add as she puts together the dressing. Add the tuna if you are serving this salad as a main dish.

3   *ounces unsalted sun-dried tomatoes*
2   *cloves garlic, peeled and minced*
1/2 *cup balsamic vinegar*
2   *tablespoons olive oil*
2   *teaspoons Italian seasoning*
2   *teaspoons grated Parmesan cheese*
1   *sweet red pepper, seeded and thinly sliced*
1   *yellow pepper, seeded and thinly sliced*
1   *cucumber, sliced*
1   *head romaine lettuce*
1   *(6 1/2-ounce) can water-packed tuna, drained and flaked (optional)*

Soak tomatoes for 30 minutes in enough warm water to cover. Drain and pat dry. Reserve. Place garlic, vinegar, olive oil, Italian seasoning, and Parmesan in a serving bowl. Add the tomatoes and combine well. Add the peppers and cucumbers and stir. Wash the romaine, pat or spin dry, and tear into bite-size portions. Add to salad bowl. Toss just before serving. If you are using tuna, add it just before serving and toss.

Per serving (including tuna):
162 calories; 13 gms. protein;
18 gms. carbohydrates; 6 gms. fat;
13 mgs. cholesterol; 162 mgs. sodium

Whenever we are together for a meal, Leanne and I make Romaine, Pepper, and Sun-Dried Tomato Salad. Since she loves sun-dried tomatoes, I take my favorite fresh tomatoes, slice them, and dry them. This way they are always on hand when Leanne is home, and the salad has a garden-fresh taste year-round.

SUN-DRIED TOMATO AND BOW-TIE PASTA SALAD WITH ALMONDS

PAREVE • SERVES 6

6   unsalted sun-dried tomatoes, cut
        into quarters or 2 medium fresh
        tomatoes, diced
2   tablespoons red wine vinegar
1/4 cup chopped fresh basil
2   tablespoons olive oil
2   tablespoons unsalted pareve
        margarine
1   clove garlic, peeled and minced
1 1/2 cups fresh bread crumbs
8   ounces dry bow-tie pasta
2   cups shredded cabbage
1/2 cup blanched, slivered almonds,
        toasted (see note)
     Basil leaves (garnish)

Cook pasta in boiling water for 9 minutes, add cabbage to boiling pasta and cook another minute. Drain. Toss bow ties and cabbage with tomato mixture, bread cubes, and toasted almonds. Garnish with basil leaves. Serve immediately.

Note: To toast almonds, heat a large skillet. Add nuts and cook until slightly browned. Remove from pan immediately.

Per serving: 305 calories; 8 gms. protein; 38 gms. carbohydrates; 14 gms. fat; 0 mgs. cholesterol; 54 mgs. sodium

---

EASY PICKLED BEETS

PAREVE • SERVES 6

2   pounds raw beets
1/2 cup apple cider vinegar
2   tablespoons sugar
2   teaspoons chopped fresh dill or
        1 teaspoon dried dill weed
1   sweet onion, thinly sliced

Wash beets and place in a 6- to 8-quart pot with enough water to cover. Bring to a boil, lower heat to medium, cover, and cook for 30 minutes or until tender. Drain, saving 1 cup of liquid. Peel and slice beets uniformly thick, about 1/4 inch. Place reserved beet liquid, vinegar, sugar, and dill in a bowl. Add sliced beets and onion. Cover and refrigerate until serving.

Per serving: 89 calories; 3 gms. protein; 22 gms. carbohydrates; 0 gms. fat; 0 mgs. cholesterol; 110 mgs. sodium

---

CUCUMBER AND ONION SALAD IN YOGURT DILL DRESSING

DAIRY • SERVES 4 TO 6

This recipe is better when prepared ahead and allowed to marinate in the refrigerator several hours or overnight.

2   cucumbers
1   cup thinly sliced onion
1/4 cup nonfat plain yogurt
1   tablespoon apple cider vinegar
1   tablespoon water
1   tablespoon finely chopped fresh dill
        or 1 1/2 teaspoons dried dill weed

Wash cucumbers and peel if they are waxed. Slice thin. Combine all ingredients in a small bowl. Cover and refrigerate until serving time.

Per serving (based on 6 servings): 28 calories; 1 gm. protein; 6 gms. carbohydrates; 0 gms. fat; 0 mgs. cholesterol; 11 mgs. sodium

---

Sun-Dried Tomato and Bow-Tie Pasta Salad with Almonds is best if served as soon as it is ready. Although almonds have a lot of fat, they are high in monounsaturated fat and calcium. I remember my grandmom always had almonds, a nutcracker, and a bowl of fruit out whenever anyone stopped by.

Potato Kugel

Couscous with Browned Onions

Carrot Tzimmes

Candied Carrots

Passover Spinach Squares

Vicki's Hot and Spicy Tomatoes and Peppers

Buckwheat Groats (Kasha) and Bow Ties

CHAPTER IV

VEGETABLES AND SIDE DISHES

Every Friday night we had either noodle or potato kugel. Grandmom Rose was the official potato kugel maker, and she imparted her knowledge to my Aunt Anita (center) and my mother (right).

POTATO KUGEL

PAREVE • SERVES 6 (2 EACH)

My memories of potato kugel are the muffin-sized, blackened, coarsely textured, heavy kugels my grandmother prepared every Friday. I thought they were the best and I begged her to give me the recipe. She really didn't have a recipe, so I stood next to her, watched, listed all the ingredients, and measured them as they poured from her hand.

To update the recipe, I substitute egg whites for some of the eggs, omit the salt, and cut the fat.

6   **large potatoes**
1   **onion**
2   **eggs or egg substitutes**
2   **egg whites**
1/4   **cup potato flour or unbleached flour**
1/2   **teaspoon baking powder**
     Dash of pepper
1/2   **teaspoon garlic powder**
2   **teaspoons olive oil**

Preheat oven to 350°F.

Peel and finely shred the potatoes and onion. Beat the eggs and egg whites until thick. Stir in the potatoes, onions, potato flour or unbleached flour, the baking powder, pepper, and garlic powder. Oil 12 ramekins or large muffin cups with olive oil. Add the potato mixture. Bake for about 1 hour, until brown and crispy.

Per serving: 98 calories; 3 gms. protein; 18 gms. carbohydrates; 2 gms. fat; 36 mgs. cholesterol; 59 mgs. sodium

---

COUSCOUS WITH BROWNED ONIONS

PAREVE • SERVES 6

This is one of my favorite Moroccan dishes to serve with any meal. It is simple and delicious. My Moroccan friend Vicki likes to add pareve powdered chicken soup mix to her couscous.

1   **tablespoon olive oil**
2   **large onions, peeled and very finely sliced**
2   **cups water**
2   **cups couscous**
1/4   **cup chopped fresh parsley (for garnish)**

Heat oil in a large skillet. Add onion and cook 15 to 20 minutes, until softened and slightly brown on the edges. In a medium saucepan, bring water to a boil, add couscous, cover, and let stand off the heat about 10 minutes. Stir couscous with a fork. Transfer to a serving bowl and combine with the onions. Top with chopped parsley.

Per serving: 269 calories; 9 gms. protein; 52 gms. carbohydrates; 3 gms. fat; 0 mgs. cholesterol; 8 mgs. sodium

---

I still make my kugel the way grandmom did: muffin-sized and coarse-textured—only now I cut back on the cholesterol and salt.

CARROT TZIMMES

MEAT • SERVES 12

This is a sweet mixture of carrots, prunes, and sweet potatoes. Sy, my husband, says his mother used white potatoes, but my grandmother used sweet potatoes. This tastes like hers did. She also used prunes with pits, and I think they are more flavorful this way; just warn everyone about the pits.

1   tablespoon vegetable oil
1   onion, peeled and sliced
1   pound lean beef cut in 1-inch cubes
2   cups water
6   carrots, peeled and sliced, or
       12 baby carrots
3   sweet potatoes, peeled and cut
       into chunks
1   pound prunes with pits
1/2   cup brown sugar

Heat the oil in a 6- to 8-quart Dutch oven and add the onion. Sauté on low for 10 minutes until softened. Add the beef and brown on all sides. When the beef is browned, add the water, bring to a boil, lower heat to simmer, cover, and cook for 1 hour. Add the carrots, sweet potatoes, prunes, and brown sugar. Cover and cook for an hour, or until the meat is very tender and the vegetables are sweet and very soft.

Per serving: 268 calories; 14 gms. protein; 44 gms. carbohydrates; 5 gms. fat; 34 mgs. cholesterol; 46 mgs. sodium

---

CANDIED CARROTS

PAREVE • SERVES 6

This is a traditional carrot recipe that Mom prepared for all the holidays. It was always served with roasted turkey and oven-browned potatoes. If you are serving more than six, add more carrots but keep the sugar, liquid, and margarine amounts the same.

2   pounds carrots
1   cup brown sugar
1   tablespoon pareve unsalted
       margarine

Wash and scrape carrots and cut into 1/4-inch-thick rounds. Steam carrots for 20 to 30 minutes until tender. Drain and measure 1 cup of the cooking liquid. Add this liquid, the brown sugar, and margarine to a pot. Bring to a boil and stir until the margarine is melted and the sugar is dissolved. Simmer for 10 minutes. Add the carrots and cook for 10 minutes.

Per serving: 251 calories; 2 gms. protein; 58 gms. carbohydrates; 2 gms. fat; 0 mgs. cholesterol; 90 mgs. sodium

---

Grandmom Rose (above) made the best Carrot Tzimmes (opposite). While there may be some debate over whether to use white potatoes or sweet potatoes, Grandmom always used sweet potatoes, and her tzimmes was delectable.

My brother Martin (left) and I (right) have very similar tastes— we both love the spinach kugel he brings with him for seder.

PASSOVER SPINACH SQUARES

PAREVE • SERVES 6 TO 8

My brother and his family come to my house for seders and always bring a delicious spinach kugel that they purchase from an Israeli deli in New York City. This is my interpretation of that spinach kugel. I use egg whites instead of whole eggs to lower the cholesterol and fat levels. Eat it any time of the year.

$1^1/2$ *pounds fresh spinach or 3 10-ounce packages frozen spinach*
1 *tablespoon pareve margarine*
1 *leek, washed well and thinly sliced*
2 *cloves garlic, minced*
3 *egg whites*
2 *teaspoons lemon juice*
$^1/8$ *teaspoon freshly grated black pepper*

If you use fresh spinach, carefully wash and drain it, then place it and about $^1/2$ cup of water in a saucepan and cook on medium-high for several minutes, until limp. Remove from heat and cool. If using frozen spinach, cook it according to the package directions. Drain and cool.

Preheat oven to 350°F.

Place the cooked spinach in a colander, pressing out as much liquid as possible. Then chop and set aside. Melt the margarine in a saucepan or skillet and add the leek and garlic. Sauté on low for 10 minutes, until softened. Beat egg whites until foamy and white. Combine chopped spinach, leek, and egg whites. Add lemon juice and black pepper. Using pareve margarine, grease an 8- by 8-inch pan.

Pour the spinach mixture into the pan, smooth out, and bake for 35 minutes. Cool and cut into squares. You can serve this as an appetizer as well as a main dish.

Per serving (based on 6 servings): 64 calories; 5 gms. protein; 8 gms. carbohydrates; 2 gms. fat; 0 mgs. cholesterol; 121 mgs. sodium

---

VICKI'S HOT AND SPICY TOMATOES AND PEPPERS

PAREVE • MAKES 3 CUPS

This recipe is an accompaniment that goes with any dish at lunch or dinner. It is a condiment my Moroccan friends prepare and use the same way Americans use ketchup. Vicki's mother told her that sautéing the peppers is okay, too, but I prefer roasting them.

1 *green pepper*
1 *tablespoon olive oil*
2 *cloves garlic, peeled and minced*
1 *onion, peeled and chopped*
1 *(28-ounce) can no-salt added tomatoes, or 4 fresh tomatoes, chopped*
1 *jalapeño pepper, chopped*

Roast the green pepper by broiling until all sides are blackened, about 10 minutes. You may have to turn the pepper once or twice to make sure that all sides are roasted. Once all sides are blackened, remove from broiler and place in a paper bag. Close the bag and allow the pepper to cool, about 15 minutes. This process makes it easier to remove the skin. Remove the pepper and hold it under running water to remove the blackened skin. Core and slice the pepper. Reserve.

Heat the oil and add the garlic and onion; sauté 10 to 15 minutes. Add the tomatoes. Use fresh tomatoes only if they are tasty and in season; otherwise, use canned. Cook very slowly on low heat for about an hour. Add reserved green pepper and chopped jalapeño pepper and continue cooking until very thick, about 10 more minutes.

Per 1/2 cup serving: 76 calories; 2 gms. protein; 13 gms. carbohydrates; 3 gms. fat; 0 mgs. cholesterol; 19 mgs. sodium

---

BUCKWHEAT GROATS (KASHA) AND BOW TIES

PAREVE • SERVES 6

This reminds me of home—and brisket. If serving without meat or gravy, some pareve powdered chicken soup mix can be added to the cooking water for extra flavor.

1	tablespoon olive oil
1/2	cup chopped onion
1	egg, beaten, or 1 egg white, unbeaten
1	cup whole or medium buckwheat groats
2	cups boiling water
2	cups dry bow-tie noodles

Heat the oil in a medium saucepan. Add onion and sauté on low until soft, about 10 minutes. With a fork, combine the egg and buckwheat groats in a bowl. Add to the onion in the sauté pan and mix until the buckwheat kernels are separated and somewhat dry. Add the boiling water to the buckwheat. Mix well, cover, and cook on low heat for 10 minutes. Meanwhile, cook the noodles according to package directions. When the noodles are cooked, combine with the cooked buckwheat.

Per serving: 195 calories; 7 gms. protein; 33 gms. carbohydrates; 5 gms. fat; 52 mgs. cholesterol; 18 mgs. sodium

---

Buckwheat is a popular Russian grain that Jews like cousin Nathalie's paternal grandfather brought here from their homeland.

Salmon Patties

Baked Haddock with Curried Yogurt Sauce

Baked Flounder with Cheese, Mushrooms, and Rice

Broiled Salmon with Red Pepper and Cucumber Relish

Chicken Cacciatore and Pasta

Baked Turkey Balls with Cabbage and Cranberries

Tuna with Garlic Mustard

Lithuanian Cabbage and Noodles

Moroccan Vegetable and Chicken Stew

Cholent

Middle Eastern Mini Lamb Balls with Eggplant and Rice

Aunt Anita's Beef Brisket

Leanne's Angel Hair Pasta with Tomato Sauce and Peas

Mike's Black Bean Chili

Falafel

Lemon Chicken with Capers and Pine Nuts

Turkey Cutlets with Peppers, Mushrooms, Onions, and Wine

Ground Turkey and Veggie Burgers

Pasta with Tuna, Artichokes, and Mushrooms

Aunt Doris's Noodle Kugel

Vegetable Lasagne

Sweet Pepper and Mushroom Frittata

Savory Vegetable and Noodle Kugel

Broccoli Rabe, Orecchiette, and Parmesan Cheese

CHAPTER V

ENTREES

An entree is generally thought to be beef, poultry, or fish. When someone asks, "What's for dinner?" they expect an answer that fits into one of these categories. Most people, though, are cutting down on the amount of animal protein they eat and increasing the amount of fruits, grains, and vegetables. So now when someone asks, "What's for dinner?" you can reply, "Pasta with Tuna, Artichokes, and Mushrooms."

Since Americans eat so much protein, I have included many vegetarian entrees, and I have modified some traditional dishes. I use fish, such as red salmon, tuna (fresh or white solid packed), sardines, mackerel, anchovies, herring, and whitefish, that come from deep, clean ocean waters; these fish also are the highest in Omega 3 fatty acids, which are useful in lowering the risk of heart disease and stroke. Cod, haddock, and flounder contain less Omega 3 fatty acids, but their low fat content makes them healthy dining. Most fresh salmon is farm-raised so there is no question about contaminants.

Sy and his family often went to Belmar, New Jersey, for a day of fishing. Aboard are: Sy, his brother Stuart, father Milt, Uncle Phil, and friends. I don't know if they ever caught anything.

SALMON PATTIES
DAIRY • SERVES 6

My mom always had a can of salmon in the cupboard to prepare these patties. They were a quick and easy dinner, and we used to eat leftovers dipped in ketchup for a snack. Make sure the bones are crushed, and include them for extra calcium in your diet. Because salmon is a large ocean fish, it is healthier than some of the smaller coastal fish.

- 1 (1-pound) can red or pink salmon
- 2 egg whites
- 2 cups oat flakes or bran flakes cereal or 1 cup bread crumbs
- 1/4 cup minced onion
- 1/4 cup 1-percent milk
- 2 tablespoons unbleached or whole wheat flour
- 1/8 teaspoon freshly ground black pepper
- 1 tablespoon corn or canola oil

Drain the salmon. Flake it and crush the bones in a large bowl. Add the egg whites, cereal or bread crumbs, onion, milk, flour, and pepper. Combine well, and form the mixture into 6 large patties. Sauté the patties in the oil in an iron or Teflon-coated pan until browned on both sides, about 10 minutes.

Per serving: 159 calories; 15 gms. protein; 10 gms. carbohydrates; 6 gms. fat; 34 mgs. cholesterol; 444 mgs. sodium

BAKED HADDOCK WITH CURRIED YOGURT SAUCE

DAIRY • SERVES 6

1	tablespoon olive oil
1	zucchini, sliced
1/4	cup finely chopped onion
1	teaspoon curry powder
	Dash of black pepper
18	ounces haddock, filleted
1/2	cup plain nonfat yogurt
2	teaspoons minced chives
1	teaspoon flour or cornstarch
2	tablespoons dry, fine, whole grain bread crumbs

Heat olive oil in a large skillet. Add zucchini, onion, curry powder, and black pepper. Stir, then cook for 8 minutes, or until vegetables are softened.

Preheat oven to 400°F. Place haddock in an 8-inch square glass baking dish. Place the vegetables over the fish. Combine the yogurt, chives, and flour or cornstarch. Pour this sauce over the vegetables. Sprinkle with bread crumbs and bake for 15 to 20 minutes or until the fish is white.

Per serving: 142 calories; 22 gms. protein; 5 gms. carbohydrates; 3 gms. fat; 63 mgs. cholesterol; 105 mgs. sodium

---

BAKED FLOUNDER WITH CHEESE, MUSHROOMS, AND RICE

DAIRY • SERVES 6

6	flounder fillets (1 1/2 pounds total)
6	tablespoons minced onion
1	teaspoon fresh dill
	Dash of freshly gound black pepper
1	cup (4 ounces) shredded, low-fat, sharp cheddar cheese
1	cup dry white wine
	Paprika to taste
1	tablespoon olive oil
1	cup chopped onion
1	cup sliced mushrooms
2	cloves garlic, peeled and minced
3	cups cooked brown or basmati rice
	Parsley (for garnish)
	Lemon slices (for garnish)

Preheat oven to 350°F.

Rinse fish and pat dry. Place a fillet on a plate and spread with a tablespoon of minced onion, some dill, and black pepper. Cover with some of the cheddar cheese. Roll up the fillet starting with the narrow end. Hold the roll together by inserting a toothpick through the center. Place the roll in an 8- by 8-inch pan. Continue with the remaining 5 fillets. Pour wine over the fillets and sprinkle with paprika. Bake for 30 minutes.

While the fish is cooking, heat the olive oil in a heavy saucepan. Add onion, mushrooms, and garlic and sauté for 10 minutes until softened. Combine the cooked rice with the sautéed vegetables. Serve by spooning rice mixture onto a serving plate. Top with the flounder rolls. Garnish with parsley and lemon slices.

Per serving: 314 calories; 25 gms. protein; 28 gms. carbohydrates; 8 gms. fat; 54 mgs. cholesterol; 169 mgs. sodium

---

BROILED SALMON WITH RED PEPPER AND CUCUMBER RELISH

PAREVE • SERVES 6

1 scallion, white and green parts,
  thinly sliced
1 kirby cucumber, finely chopped
1 kiwi, peeled, sliced, and
  finely chopped
1/2 red pepper, seeded and
  finely chopped
2 tablespoons balsamic vinegar
1 teaspoon frozen apple juice
  concentrate
6 salmon steaks (1 1/2 to 2 pounds
  total)
  Kiwi slices (for garnish)
  Lemon slices (for garnish)

Combine scallion, cucumber, kiwi, and red pepper in a small bowl. Add the balsamic vinegar and apple juice. Stir and set aside. Place salmon steaks on a broiling pan. Broil 5 inches from heat for 4 minutes. Turn and broil the other side for 4 minutes, until slightly browned. Place on serving plates. Fill opening in each salmon steak with some of the relish. Garnish with parsley.

---

*Per serving: 171 calories; 24 gms.
protein; 4 gms. carbohydrates; 7 gms.
fat; 42 mgs. cholesterol; 52 mgs. sodium*

Growing up, fresh salmon was a treat for us; now canned and fresh salmon cost about the same, and lox is the treat. This Broiled Salmon with Red Pepper and Cucumber Relish is easy enough for a quick weeknight dinner, yet special enough for family gatherings.

CHICKEN CACCIATORE AND PASTA

MEAT • SERVES 6

My husband likes this recipe very much. The tomato sauce tastes delicious on the pasta.

6 chicken breast halves, skinned
  and boned
1/4 cup olive oil
1/4 pound mushrooms
2 cups finely chopped onion
1 green pepper, seeded and chopped
4 garlic cloves, peeled and minced
1/2 teaspoon dried basil
1 cup no-salt added canned tomatoes
  or tomato puree
1/4 cup dry red wine
8 ounces pasta, cooked

Sauté chicken in olive oil for 10 minutes or until golden brown on both sides. Add mushrooms, onion, green pepper, garlic, and basil. Simmer 5 minutes. Add tomatoes or puree. Bring to a boil, reduce heat, cover, and simmer for 20 minutes, stirring occasionally. Add wine and simmer 10 minutes. Serve over cooked pasta.

---

*Per serving: 465 calories;
60 gms. protein; 39 gms. carbohydrates;
16 gms. fat; 146 mgs. cholesterol;
149 mgs. sodium*

Another photograph of Sy, the fisherman. He sometimes caught flounder, which I would then bake for dinner.

Aunt Anita, who coined the term "Psèudo Prakas." Here she is with her husband, Milton, and son, Dick, when they were stationed in Joplin, Missouri.

BAKED TURKEY BALLS WITH CABBAGE AND CRANBERRIES

MEAT • SERVES 12

Aunt Anita call these "Pseudo Prakas." Prakas are stuffed cabbage rolls; the flavor of stuffed cabbage is here but there is less fat and cholesterol. There is less work, too, because the cabbage leaves do not have to be steamed and then stuffed and rolled.

2	pounds cabbage, shredded
3	pounds ground turkey
2	eggs or egg substitutes
1	cup bread crumbs
1	medium onion, shredded
1/2	green pepper, seeded and finely chopped
2	teaspoons prepared mustard
1/2	teaspoon garlic powder
1/4	teaspoon ground black pepper
1	(10-ounce) bottle low-sodium chili sauce
2/3	cup water
1	(16-ounce) can whole cranberry sauce
1	(8-ounce) can no-salt added tomato sauce

Preheat oven to 350°F.

Spread shredded cabbage in a large roasting pan. Combine turkey, eggs, bread crumbs, onion, green pepper, mustard, garlic powder, and black pepper, and shape mixture into small balls (about 36). Place these balls over the cabbage. Pour chili sauce evenly over the balls and cabbage. Fill the chili sauce bottle with the water and pour over the cabbage in the pan. Empty the cranberry sauce over the roast-ing pan, spreading it evenly over the balls. Pour the tomato sauce over the cranber-ries. Cover the roasting pan with a lid or aluminum foil and bake 1 1/2 to 2 hours or until the cabbage is softened. (Actually the longer it bakes, the better it tastes.) Serve with broad egg noodles, so that the deli-cious gravy is not wasted.

Per serving (without noodles):
294 calories; 28 gms. protein;
34 gms. carbohydrates; 5 gms. fat;
109 mgs. cholesterol; 211 mgs. sodium

TUNA WITH GARLIC MUSTARD

PAREVE • SERVES 6

1	tablespoon olive oil
2	tablespoons coarse mustard
2	tablespoons chopped parsley
1	tablespoon lime juice
2	cloves garlic, peeled and minced
6	tuna steaks, each 1 inch thick (1 1/2 to 2 pounds total)

Combine all ingredients except tuna, then coat both sides of the tuna with this mix-ture. Broil about 4 minutes per side about 5 inches from the heat.

Per serving: 118 calories; 20 gms. protein;
0.9 gm. carbohydrates; 3 gms. fat;
38 mgs. cholesterol; 100 mgs. sodium

Tuna with Garlic Mustard is a quick, healthful, and easy recipe that is perfect as a Shabbat evening meal.

Grandpa Sam and Grandmom Rose. It was from Grandmom Rose that I acquired the basis for many of the traditional dishes in my own repertoire. This Lithuanian Cabbage and Noodle recipe is a variation of hers.

LITHUANIAN CABBAGE AND NOODLES

DAIRY • SERVES 6

My grandmother combined these noodles with a scoop of cottage cheese. Complete the meal by adding salad, bread, and fruit.

4   tablespoons butter
1   large onion, peeled and thinly sliced
1   head (1 to 2 pounds) cabbage, thinly sliced
8   ounces flat egg noodles (¼ to ½ inch wide)
½   teaspoon caraway seeds

Melt butter in a large pot or skillet. Add onion and cabbage and cook on low until softened and browned, about 30 minutes. While the onions and cabbage are cooking, prepare noodles according to package directions. Drain. Add noodles and caraway seeds to cabbage mixture. Combine well. Cover pot and cook on low for about 10 minutes.

*Per serving: 267 calories;
8 gms. protein; 39 gms. carbohydrates;
10 gms. fat; 59 mgs. cholesterol;
112 mgs. sodium*

MOROCCAN VEGETABLE AND CHICKEN STEW

MEAT • SERVES 6

2   tablespoons olive oil
6   chicken breast halves
1   carrot, peeled and sliced
1   onion, peeled and sliced
½   cup water
1   teaspoon ground coriander
1   clove garlic, peeled and minced
¼   teaspoon cayenne pepper
½   teaspoon ground turmeric
1   cup cooked chick-peas
1   cup cauliflower florets
½   cup couscous
¼   cup golden raisins
½   cup hot tap water

Heat olive oil in skillet, add chicken, and cook until golden on both sides, about 15 minutes. Add carrot, onion, water, coriander, garlic, cayenne pepper, and ¼ teaspoon turmeric. Bring to a boil, lower the heat to simmer, cover, and cook for 15 minutes. Add chick-peas and cauliflower and simmer 10 more minutes. Meanwhile, place couscous, the remaining ¼ teaspoon turmeric, and raisins in a bowl. Pour the hot water over this, stir, and let stand. When ready to serve, spoon couscous onto a flat serving platter. Arrange chicken on it and top with the sauce and vegetables.

*Per serving: 395 calories;
52 gms. protein; 28 gms. carbohydrates;
8 gms. fat; 116 mgs. cholesterol;
144 mgs. sodium*

CHOLENT

MEAT • SERVES 6

Of all the foods we think of as Jewish, there are really only three that are: Matzoh, gefilte fish, and cholent. Most families had their own favorite recipe for cholent that could be kept in the oven for sixteen hours.

I had never made cholent before, but I had heard several family members talk with love and tenderness about Aunt Ann Glazier's cholent. So, I called Aunt Ann.

Most who remember her cholent (she hasn't made it in years) couldn't wait for me to try her recipe. They remembered the beans and the browned and crispy potatoes. Her son remembered her continuously adding liquid to her stoneware pot so the cholent wouldn't dry out. Though I had never made cholent, I had read various recipes that said to keep it covered until ready to be eaten. I couldn't understand how so many remembered it as brown and crispy.

Cholent really is a healthy food by today's standards; lots of vegetables, high-fiber legumes, and a little meat. So I prepared Aunt Ann's recipe. I added an onion, garlic, and bay leaves, and I removed the salt and some of the beef.

And then I served it. "This is it," they all said and finished a bowlful. It wasn't crispy, and there wasn't any left.

½ **cup large dried lima beans
    (2 cups cooked)**
½ **cup dried red kidney beans
    (2 cups cooked)**
1 **tablespoon olive oil**
1 **onion, sliced**
2 **cloves garlic, sliced**
6 **large potatoes, quartered**
¾ **pound beef flanken, fat trimmed,
    cut into 4 or 5 pieces**
6 **cups water**
2 **bay leaves
    Dash freshly ground black pepper**

Place beans in a large bowl and cover with cold water. Soak for several hours or overnight.

In a large Dutch oven or a large pot with a lid, heat the oil. Add the onion and garlic and sauté for 10 minutes on low until softened.

Drain the beans and add to the pot along with the remaining ingredients. Cover the pot and place it in a 250°F oven. The cholent should remain in the oven for 10 to 12 hours, but can cook up to 16 hours. By the time the dish is served, most of the water will be absorbed and everything will be very tender.

If you prefer, cook for 4 hours at 350°F.

Per serving: 336 calories; 20 gms. protein; 46 gms. carbohydrates; 8 gms. fat; 28 mgs. cholesterol; 51 mgs. sodium

Potatoes are an integral part of cholent. Although the potatoes in my cholent never get crispy, they are delicious just the same.

MIDDLE EASTERN MINI LAMB BALLS WITH EGGPLANT AND RICE

MEAT • SERVES 6

I got the idea for this dish from my Moroccan friends, Rima and Vicki Cohen. Rima made me a dish of mini beef balls, mushrooms, and chicken livers in gravy served over puff pastry shells. I made this lower-fat, salt-free recipe using lamb.

1   tablespoon olive oil
1   clove garlic, peeled and minced
1   onion, peeled and finely chopped
1/2 green pepper, seeded and chopped
1   small (1 pound) eggplant, peeled
        and cut into 1/4-inch cubes
1   cup water
1   bay leaf
1   pound ground lamb
1   teaspoon ground coriander
1/2 teaspoon cumin
1/2 teaspoon ground turmeric
1/4 teaspoon black pepper
2   tablespoons lemon juice
1/4 cup chopped parsley (for garnish)
3   cups cooked rice or couscous

Heat oil in heavy 12-inch frying pan. Add garlic, onion, and green pepper. Sauté for 10 minutes on medium-low heat. Add eggplant, water, and bay leaf. Cover, and cook for 10 minutes. Roll ground lamb into tiny balls, about 1/2 to 1 teaspoon each. Add to frying pan, in batches, as you form them. When all balls are added, sprinkle the coriander, cumin, turmeric, and pepper over the top, cover, and continue cooking for 15 minutes. Stir well, add lemon juice, and stir again. The eggplant and water should form a thick sauce. Sprinkle with chopped parsley and serve over cooked rice or couscous.

Per serving (with rice): 268 calories; 19 gms. protein; 31 gms. carbohydrates; 8 gms. fat; 53 mgs. cholesterol; 67 mgs. sodium

---

AUNT ANITA'S BEEF BRISKET

MEAT • SERVES 6

2 to 3 pounds lean beef brisket
2   onions, peeled and sliced
2   carrots, peeled and sliced
1   stalk celery, sliced
2   bay leaves
1   (8-ounce) can no-salt added
        tomato sauce

Place the beef brisket in the bottom of a 4- to 6-quart Dutch oven with a lid. Add the onions, carrots, celery, and bay leaves. Cover with the tomato sauce and then fill the empty can of tomato sauce with water and add this to the pot. Bring the liquid to a boil over high heat, lower heat, cover, and cook on top of the stove for 2 hours or until the brisket is tender. The brisket can be made a day in advance and refrigerated to allow the fat to harden. Discard any fat that forms. Reheat, slice the meat, and serve it separately from the gravy.

Per serving (unskimmed): 256 calories; 28 gms. protein; 10 gms. carbohydrates; 11 gms. fat; 82 mgs. cholesterol; 90 mgs. sodium

---

LEANNE'S ANGEL HAIR PASTA WITH TOMATO SAUCE AND PEAS

DAIRY • SERVES 6

My daughter, Leanne, invented this dish, and it immediately became her favorite. Because angel hair pasta cooks so quickly and the sauce can come from a bottle, it is fast and healthy.

1   tablespoon olive oil
1   clove garlic, peeled and minced
1   (26-ounce jar) marinara sauce or
        Anita's Own Tomato Sauce
        (see page 91)
1   tablespoon Parmesan cheese
2   tablespoons whole milk or part skim
        ricotta cheese
1   cup frozen, thawed peas or broccoli
1   pound angel hair pasta, cooked

Heat olive oil in a saucepan. Add garlic and sauté until softened. Add marinara sauce or Anita's Own Tomato Sauce, and Parmesan and ricotta cheeses. Stir and bring to a simmer. Add peas or broccoli and cook until heated through. Serve over angel hair pasta.

Per serving (using whole milk ricotta): 391 calories; 14 gms. protein; 74 gms. carbohydrates; 5 gms. fat; 3 mgs. cholesterol; 62 mgs. sodium

---

MIKE'S BLACK BEAN CHILI

DAIRY • SERVES 6

When my son, Mike, has dinner guests, he prepares this chili. He passed all of his hints on to me: Smash the garlic and jalapeños with a chef's knife or your fist so they can be thrown into the vegetables without mincing. Jarred hot jalapeño peppers can be used if fresh jalapeños are not available. Mike uses dried coriander if fresh coriander (cilantro) is not available. I omitted the salt and used light Monterey Jack cheese and light sour cream.

- 2   cups dried black beans
- 6   cups water
- 1   tablespoon cumin
       (ground or seeds)
- 1   teaspoon dried oregano
- 1   teaspoon dried thyme
- 1   teaspoon dried marjoram
- 1   tablespoon olive oil
- 1   medium onion, finely chopped
- 1/2 green pepper, chopped
- 1   clove garlic, smashed
       Dash Tabasco
- 2   teaspoons paprika
- 2   cups chopped fresh tomatoes or 1
       (16-ounce) can no-salt added
       tomatoes with their juice,
       chopped
- 2   fresh or canned jalapeño peppers,
       minced
- 1   tablespoon chopped fresh cilantro
       or 1 1/2 teaspoons dried coriander
- 4   ounces shredded low-fat Monterey
       Jack cheese
- 1/3 cup light sour cream (for garnish)
- 1/4 cup finely chopped scallions, white
       and green parts (for garnish)

Rinse the beans and remove any impurities. Put the beans in a 4- to 6-quart pot, cover with water, and soak overnight. Or, to speed up this soaking process, cover the beans with boiling water and let stand, covered, for one hour. Drain beans. Put beans back into the pot with 6 cups of water, bring to a boil, lower heat, cover, and cook on low to medium heat for one hour or until tender. Drain beans and save 1/2 cup of liquid.

Combine the cumin, oregano, thyme, and marjoram in a small baking dish and toast at 350°F for 10 minutes. Heat the oil in a skillet at medium-low heat. Add the onion, green pepper, and garlic and sauté for 10 minutes. Place 1/2 cup reserved bean liquid, toasted herbs, sautéed vegetables, Tabasco, paprika, tomatoes, jalapeño peppers, cilantro, and beans in a pot. Bring the mixture to a simmer and cook for 10 minutes.

To serve, place some of the shredded Monterey Jack in the bottom of an individual serving bowl, place chili over the cheese, and top with a tablespoon of light sour cream and chopped scallions.

Per serving: 353 calories; 21 gms. protein; 50 gms. carbohydrates; 9 gms. fat; 10 mgs. cholesterol; 76 mgs. sodium

Beans are increasingly being recognized as an important part of a healthy diet. What better way to enjoy them than in a delicious spicy bowl of chili?

FALAFEL

PAREVE, WITHOUT YOGURT • MAKES 24
FALAFEL; 3 OR 4 PER SERVING

In Israel, falafel are made from chick-peas that are ground, seasoned, shaped into small patties, deep-fried, and served in a pita. Greeks prepare their falafel with broad beans. Any bean or any combination of beans will do. This falafel is sautéed in a little oil until it is browned on both sides. No salt is added.

3/4	*cup dried white beans or chick-peas (2 cups cooked)*
2 to 3	*scallions, white and green parts, finely chopped*
1	*clove garlic, peeled and minced*
2	*tablespoons chopped parsley*
1/2	*teaspoon cumin*
1/2	*teaspoon coriander*
	Dash cayenne pepper
1/4	*teaspoon baking powder*
	Bulgur (to thicken)
2	*tablespoons vegetable oil*
4	*individual pita breads*
	Lettuce, tomato, cucumber, scallion, and yogurt or tahini dressing

To cook dried beans, boil 1 quart water. Add raw beans, cover pot, and remove from heat. Soak 1 hour. After 1 hour, drain beans and return to pot. Add a quart of water, bring to a boil, cover, and cook on medium-high for 1 hour or until tender.

Drain the beans, reserving the liquid. Add beans to food processor and process until smooth. Bean liquid can be added if mixture is too thick. Spoon into a bowl. Add all falafel ingredients except the bulgur and oil. Set aside. Add bulgur, if necessary, to thicken. Add more bean liquid if mixture is too thick. To shape the patties, take an amount the size of a walnut and form it into a patty about 1½ inches in diameter. As patties are formed, sauté in hot oil, turning once, until they are a rich golden brown on all sides. Serve 3 to 4 in a pita with lettuce, chopped tomato, cucumber, and scallion. Top with yogurt or tahini dressing. (To make tahini dressing, process tahini with lemon juice and garlic until it is thin.)

Per serving (3 per serving; falafel only): 113 calories; 5 gms. protein; 13 gms. carbohydrates; 5 gms. fat; 0 mgs. cholesterol; 19 mgs. sodium

---

LEMON CHICKEN WITH CAPERS AND PINE NUTS

MEAT • SERVES 6

Serve this chicken with steamed broccoli and drizzle some of the pan juices over it. I have made this recipe with chicken breasts with or without the bone and it is wonderful either way. If you cook it with the skin, remove the skin before eating.

1/4	*cup pine nuts*
1	*tablespoon olive oil*
6	*chicken breast halves, skinned and boned*
1/2	*cup dry white wine*
1½	*tablespoons lemon juice*
1	*tablespoon capers*

Toast the pine nuts in a 400°F oven until lightly browned. Reserve.

Heat the olive oil in a large skillet. Add the chicken breasts and sauté about 5 minutes until golden. Turn and cook on the other side until golden brown and cooked through. Transfer chicken to a platter. Pour out and discard any fat from the pan. Add the wine to the pan and bring it to a boil. Scrape the pan with a wooden spoon and continue cooking until the wine is reduced to about ¼ cup. Add the lemon juice, capers, and toasted pine nuts. Pour sauce over the chicken.

Per serving: 355 calories; 55 gms. protein; 2 gms. carbohydrates; 12 gms. fat; 146 mgs. cholesterol; 157 mgs. sodium

---

Lemon Chicken with Capers and Pine Nuts makes a delicious, quick, everyday meal, one that is special enough to serve on Shabbat.

My Uncle Mickey was the official burger maker in the family.

TURKEY CUTLETS WITH PEPPERS, MUSHROOMS, ONIONS, AND WINE

MEAT • SERVES 6

My Aunt Anita got this recipe years ago. It is a wonderful dish to serve to company because it can be prepared in advance and reheated in the oven thirty minutes before serving time. In Aunt Anita's version, the boned chicken cutlets were dipped in egg and bread crumbs, and then sautéed in oil, but I eliminated these stages. She also sprinkled pareve powdered chicken soup mix over it; I eliminated this to cut the extra salt.

1 1/2   pounds turkey cutlets
1   large onion, peeled and
        thinly sliced
1   red pepper, seeded and
        thinly sliced
1   green pepper, seeded and
        thinly sliced
1/2   pound mushrooms, thinly sliced
1/3   cup dry white wine
1   teaspoon Italian seasoning

Preheat oven to 350°F.

Cut the turkey cutlets into 3- to 4-ounce portions. (They are usually cut into 6- to 8-ounce portions, so they need to be cut in half.) Lay them in an 8-inch square baking dish. Cover the turkey with the onion, peppers, and mushrooms. Pour in the white wine and sprinkle the Italian seasoning over all. Cover and bake for 30 minutes.

This can be prepared in advance and refrigerated until 30 minutes before serving time, or it can be baked the day before or early in the day, and then refrigerated and reheated at serving time.

Per serving: 195 calories; 36 gms. protein; 5 gms. carbohydrates; 1 gm. fat; 95 mgs. cholesterol; 76 mgs. sodium

GROUND TURKEY AND VEGGIE BURGERS

MEAT • SERVES 6

These burgers are equally as good prepared on the grill as they are broiled. The vegetables add vitamins and fiber and "stretch" the turkey.

1 1/4   pounds ground turkey
2   carrots, peeled and shredded
1   small onion, peeled and
        finely chopped
2   cloves garlic, minced
1   egg white

Combine all the ingredients in a bowl. Mix well and form into 6 large burgers. Place on broiling pan or grill. Broil or grill for 8 minutes on each side for well-done burgers. Serve on buns with lettuce, sliced tomato, and mustard.

Per serving (burger only): 132 calories; 22 gms. protein; 4 gms. carbohydrates; 3 gms. fat; 62 mgs. cholesterol; 84 mgs. sodium

Today, Ground Turkey and Veggie Burgers allow us to feel less guilty about loving burgers so much.

PASTA WITH TUNA, ARTICHOKES, AND MUSHROOMS

DAIRY • SERVES 6

This recipe was one my daughter, Leanne, enjoyed when she had dinner at her friend Tony Goldberg's. The delicious and quick pasta sauce can be served over an individual portion of cooked spaghetti and then topped with parsley and grated Parmesan. Any remaining sauce can be refrigerated and heated the next day.

2	*tablespoons olive oil*
1	*medium onion, peeled and chopped*
2	*cloves garlic, peeled and minced*
8	*mushrooms, thinly sliced*
1	*(13³/₄-ounce) can artichoke hearts*
1	*(12¹/₂-ounce) can solid white tuna packed in water*
1	*teaspoon Italian seasoning*
1	*teaspoon chopped fresh basil or ¹/₂ teaspoon dry*
¹/₂	*teaspoon celery seed*
1	*pound thin spaghetti*
4	*quarts water*
¹/₃	*cup chopped parsley (for garnish)*
¹/₃	*cup grated Parmesan cheese (for garnish)*

Pasta with Tuna, Artichokes, and Mushrooms has become a household staple not only at the Goldbergs', but at my house as well.

Place olive oil in a 10- to 12-inch skillet over medium heat. Add onion, garlic, and mushrooms and sauté about 10 minutes, until vegetables are softened. Do not brown. Drain the artichoke hearts and cut in quarters; add to skillet. Drain tuna and break into bite-size chunks; add to skillet. Add Italian seasoning, basil, and celery seed. Continue sautéing for about 5 minutes until the tuna and artichoke hearts are heated through. While tuna mixture is heating, bring 4 quarts water to a boil for spaghetti. Cook spaghetti about 7 minutes and drain. Place in serving bowl. Toss with tuna mixture. Serve garnished with parsley and cheese.

---

*Per serving: 432 calories;
30 gms. protein; 64 gms. carbohydrates;
9 gms. fat; 27 mgs. cholesterol;
375 mgs. sodium*

Here's Aunt Doris in her kitchen preparing kugel for a family gathering. Although she vows that she will never change her recipe, I've modified it to be healthier.

Aunt Doris's Noodle Kugel

DAIRY • MAKES 30 SQUARES

My Uncle Bernie's family ate kugel for dessert or served it with tea. In my family it was served as a side dish. When I asked Aunt Doris what food she thought of as a Jewish food, she said, "Just a minute," ran to her freezer, and brought out a frozen kugel. When I took a sample of this to my parents, Mom heated it in the microwave and Dad took out the low-fat frozen yogurt and gave everyone a big scoop. I asked Aunt Doris if she modifies her kugel now to be more healthy and she said, "No! I don't want to change a good recipe."

To lower the fat, I use low-fat cottage cheese, light sour cream, and light cream cheese. Then I eliminate the salt, butter, and sugar in the topping. The fat and calories can be reduced even more by substituting yogurt cheese or fat-free sour cream for sour cream.

1/2	*pound medium noodles, cooked*
12	*ounces low-fat cottage cheese*
1/2	*pint light sour cream*
1/4	*pound melted butter or margarine*
1	*teaspoon vanilla*
2	*tablespoons lemon juice*
3/4	*cup sugar*
1/2	*cup raisins*
1/2	*teaspoon cinnamon*
1/4	*pound light cream cheese*
4	*eggs, separated*
4	*tablespoons graham cracker crumbs*

Preheat oven to 350°F.

In a 9- by 13-inch pan, combine all ingredients, except egg whites and graham cracker crumbs. Beat the egg whites until they hold soft peaks. Fold into pan. Top with graham cracker crumbs. Bake, uncovered, for 50 minutes.

Per serving: 126 calories; 4 gms. protein; 14 gms. carbohydrates; 6 gms. fat; 48 mgs. cholesterol; 110 mgs. sodium

---

Here's a version of Aunt Doris's Noodle Kugel that's lower in fat and smaller in size.

DAIRY • SERVES 9

2	*eggs*
1	*cup light ricotta*
1	*cup nonfat sour cream*
1/2	*teaspoon vanilla extract*
2/3	*cup sugar*
1/2	*pound fine egg noodles, cooked*
1	*tablespoon sugar*
1/2	*teaspoon cinnamon*

Preheat oven to 350°F.

Beat eggs in a bowl. Stir in ricotta and nonfat sour cream. Mix well. Add the vanilla, sugar, and cooked egg noodles. Lightly oil an 8- by 8-inch square pan. Pour in noodle mixture. Combine sugar and cinnamon and dust over top. Bake for 45 minutes.

Per serving: 242 calories; 10 gms. protein; 39 gms. carbohydrates; 4.3 gms. fat; 84 mgs. cholesterol; 87 mgs. sodium

---

VEGETABLE LASAGNE

DAIRY • SERVES 12 TO 16

Developing this recipe was an interesting project. I wanted to bake the lasagne in a microwave, and I wanted to be able to layer all the ingredients uncooked. I gave some to my sister-in-law, Carol, to taste and she liked it very much, but felt the vegetables were al dente and the pasta a bit pasty. So I added more liquid and increased the cooking time. It can be oven-baked or baked in the microwave.

28 to 30 ounces (about 4 cups)
marinara or Anita's Own
Tomato Sauce
8 uncooked lasagne noodles
1 (10-ounce) package chopped
frozen broccoli, thawed
and drained
1 zucchini, sliced
1 yellow zucchini, sliced
1/2 pound mushrooms, sliced
1 onion, peeled and
thinly sliced
1 (10-ounce) package chopped
frozen spinach, thawed
and drained
2 cups skim milk ricotta cheese
1 egg or 2 egg whites
2 cups shredded skim milk
mozzarella cheese
1/4 teaspoon black pepper
1/2 teaspoon dried basil
1/2 teaspoon garlic powder
1/2 teaspoon dried oregano
1/4 cup grated Parmesan cheese

Preheat oven to 350°F.

In a 9- by 13-inch pan, layer half of the marinara or Anita's Own Tomato Sauce, 4 uncooked lasagne noodles, half the broccoli, half the zucchini, half the yellow zucchini, half the mushrooms, half the onion, and half the spinach. Combine the ricotta cheese with the egg or egg whites and spread half of this mixture over the vegetables. Next spread half of the mozzarella over the ricotta. Repeat these layers and end with the herbs and the Parmesan cheese on top. Cover and bake in the oven for one hour or until the vegetables are tender. Uncover and bake 10 minutes to brown on top. To cook in the microwave, cover and bake on high for 8 minutes, then on medium-low for 35 to 40 minutes. Let stand 15 minutes before serving.

*Per serving: 205 calories;
15 gms. protein; 22 gms. carbohydrates;
7 gms. fat; 41 mgs. cholesterol;
222 mgs. sodium*

ANITA'S OWN TOMATO SAUCE

PAREVE • MAKES 1 QUART

The secret to this sauce is using fresh garden tomatoes. If you can't get tasty fresh ones, use canned.

1 tablespoon olive oil
1 medium onion, peeled
and chopped
2 cloves garlic, peeled
and minced
8 to 10 fresh tomatoes, peeled, seeded,
and quartered or 2 quarts
no-salt added canned
tomatoes
1/4 cup chopped parsley
1 teaspoon oregano
1 teaspoon dried basil or
1 tablespoon chopped fresh

Heat oil in a large, heavy pot. Add onion and garlic and sauté on low heat for 15 minutes until softened. Add tomatoes and parsley and cook on medium-high. Continue to cook at a low boil until the sauce is reduced by half; this will take about 30 minutes. Add the oregano and basil and cook 5 minutes more.

*Per 1/4 cup: 24 calories; 0.7 gm. protein;
4 gms. carbohydrates; 1 gm. fat;
0 mgs. cholesterol; 6 mgs. sodium*

SWEET PEPPER AND MUSHROOM FRITTATA

DAIRY • SERVES 6

This recipe makes six individual frittatas, but it can easily make one large frittata or the recipe can be cut to make only one portion. Whole eggs can be used or, to reduce the fat, use egg substitute.

2	tablespoons plus 2 teaspoons olive oil
1	teaspoon dried thyme
2	cloves garlic, peeled and minced
2	teaspoons lemon juice
1¹/₂	teaspoons coarse mustard
6	scallions, white and green parts, cut into 3-inch lengths
12	mushrooms, sliced
1	red pepper, seeded and thinly sliced
1	green pepper, seeded and thinly sliced
4	tablespoons Parmesan cheese
6	eggs or egg substitutes
6	egg whites

Individual frittatas are a very impressive brunch entree, and each person can request his or her favorite ingredients. Sweet peppers and mushrooms are a delicious frittata combination, but add any vegetables you like.

Heat 2 teaspoons of olive oil in a 10-inch skillet. Add thyme, garlic, lemon juice, and mustard. Stir to combine. Add vegetables and stir to coat. Sauté on medium-low heat until the vegetables are softened, about 10 minutes. Turn off heat and reserve. Preheat the broiler. In a 6-inch cast iron skillet (or a pan that can be used on top of the stove and in the oven), heat a teaspoon of the remaining olive oil. In a bowl, beat 2 teaspoons of the Parmesan cheese, 1 egg, and 1 egg white. Add this mixture to the heated oil. Add ¹/₆ of the cooked vegetable mixture to the top of the egg mixture. After a few minutes the egg around the edge of the pan will begin to cook and change texture. Put the pan 5 to 6 inches from the broiler. The top will puff and become golden after 3 to 4 minutes.

Remove the pan from the oven and slide the frittata out onto a serving plate. Continue with the remaining oil, eggs, cheese, and vegetables until all of the frittatas are prepared.

To prepare one large frittata, sauté and reserve the vegetables. Lightly oil a 12-inch skillet. Beat the egg and egg whites until foamy. Add the Parmesan cheese. Pour into the prepared pan and cook. Add vegetables. Broil the top, remove from oven, and cut into 6 wedges.

Per serving (half eggs and half whites): 178 calories; 12 gms. protein; 4 gms. carbohydrates; 13 gms. fat; 216 mgs. cholesterol; 214 mgs. sodium

SAVORY VEGETABLE AND NOODLE KUGEL

DAIRY • SERVES 6

I am one of those people who clips recipes from newspapers and magazines. At this point, with the collection I have, I could never try them all. One I did try was a recipe that appeared in *Jewish Living Magazine* in 1979. The recipe was sent in by M. Coffey of New York City and won third prize. I have modified it and served it many times—even prepared it for two hundred at my daughter's bat mitzvah. I use all low-fat products, no salt, and much less oil than the original recipe calls for.

1/2	*pound broad egg or spinach noodles, cooked*
2 to 3	*stalks broccoli*
1/4	*head cauliflower*
1	*tablespoon vegetable oil*
1	*medium onion, peeled and chopped*
1	*cup sliced mushrooms*
1/2	*pound low-fat cottage cheese*
1	*cup shredded low-fat Cheddar cheese*
1/2	*teaspoon garlic powder*
1/2	*teaspoon dry mustard*

Preheat oven to 350°F.

Coarsely chop the broccoli and cauliflower and steam them together for 4 to 5 minutes. Drain and reserve. Heat the oil in a skillet. Add the onion and mushrooms and sauté for 10 minutes on medium-low heat. Combine all ingredients, except 1/2 cup of the cheddar cheese, in a lightly oiled, nonstick, sprayed, or Teflon-coated 9- by 9-inch square pan. Top with the reserved 1/2 cup of shredded Cheddar cheese. Bake for 30 minutes or until the cheese bubbles and browns.

Per serving: 301 calories;
19 gms. protein; 39 gms. carbohydrates;
9 gms. fat; 52 mgs. cholesterol;
284 mgs. sodium

BROCCOLI RABE, ORECCHIETTE, AND PARMESAN CHEESE

DAIRY • SERVES 6

1	*cup water*
1	*bunch broccoli rabe, cleaned and chopped into 2-inch sections*
4	*cups raw orecchiette or pasta curl noodles*
2	*tablespoons grated Parmesan cheese Parmesan cheese (for garnish)*

Bring 1 cup water to boil in a saucepan. Add the broccoli rabe, turn the heat to medium-high, cover, and boil for 5 minutes; the stems will be slightly tender and still green. Pour into a colander and drain.

While the broccoli rabe is cooking, cook the orecchiette according to package directions. Remove broccoli rabe from the colander and place in a large serving bowl. Drain pasta and add to the bowl with the broccoli rabe. Toss with the Parmesan and serve immediately with extra Parmesan on the side.

Per serving: 263 calories; 11 gms. protein; 51 gms. carbohydrates; 2 gms. fat; 2 mgs. cholesterol; 55 mgs. sodium

---

After a hard day at work, serve Broccoli Rabe, Orecchiette, and Parmesan Cheese with some Italian bread and a big portion of fruit salad and yogurt.

CHAPTER VI

BREADS

Saul Kivert originated this Challah recipe.

CHALLAH

PAREVE • MAKES 2 LOAVES

I use a recipe that originally came from Maxine Tannenbaum Kline and her father, Saul Kivert. I had been to a family bar mitzvah where they had presented the guests with a giant challah they had made for the blessing.

2	ounces compressed yeast or 2 packages active dry yeast
1¼	cups lukewarm water
¼	cup sugar
⅓	cup vegetable oil
½	teaspoon salt
3	eggs or egg substitutes, beaten (reserve 1 tablespoon for brushing on top)
5 to 6¼	cups unbleached flour
1	tablespoon honey
	Poppy seeds (optional)

In a large mixing bowl, dissolve the yeast in the lukewarm water, mixing with a spoon to combine. When thoroughly dissolved, add the sugar, oil, salt, and eggs, mixing well. Gradually add 4 cups of flour, beating it into the mixture. The batter will be lumpy and runny. Add more flour, using a spoon to combine, until the dough is too thick to beat. The dough will be stiff but sticky. Turn the dough out onto a floured board. With floured hands, knead the dough for 5 to 10 minutes, adding flour as necessary to make a smooth and stretchy dough. Place the dough in an oiled bowl, turning once to coat the dough with oil. Cover the bowl with a cloth and allow to rise in a warm place until it doubles in bulk; this will take about 1 hour. Punch the dough down and divide it into two parts. Divide each part into 3 equal pieces. Roll these pieces into strips about 12 inches long. Pinch 3 strips together at the top and then braid them. Place the braided loaf in an oiled 9- by 5-inch loaf pan. Repeat with the other 3 strips. Cover the 2 loaves and let rise for ½ hour or until the dough rises to the top of the pan. Combine the reserved egg with the honey and brush this mixture over the loaves. Sprinkle with poppy seeds, if desired. Preheat oven to 375°F. Bake bread for 30 minutes. Cool for 20 minutes and remove from the pan.

Variations:

1. To make raisin challah, knead ½ cup of raisins into the dough after the dough has been kneaded for 5 to 10 minutes. Proceed as above.

2. Instead of baking the bread in bread pans, place the loaves on oiled baking sheets.

3. Instead of braiding the dough, shape it into two round loaves, and place them on baking sheets to rise. Bake for 30 minutes at 375°F. When golden brown, knock the bread with your knuckle, it should sound hollow. Turn the bread over and it will be browned on the bottom as well. Remove from the oven.

Per slice (15 slices per loaf): 114 calories; 3 gms. protein; 18 gms. carbohydrates; 3 gms. fat; 21 mgs. cholesterol; 42 mgs. sodium

---

Fresh-baked challah is always a welcome treat, so why serve it only on holidays or at special occasions?

When Nana (Sy's mother, Dorothy) heard anyone say they liked her Onion Rolls, she'd jump up and make them. Here she is enjoying tea (and perhaps an onion roll?) with Sy.

NANA'S ONION ROLLS

PAREVE • MAKES 12 ROLLS

These are the rolls my husband fondly calls "sybila pletzl." They are like bialys, but are a little softer and sweeter. Even though I have modified the recipe, it is still somewhat high in fat.

1	package active dry yeast
3/4	cup warm water
2	tablespoons sugar
1/2	teaspoon salt
1/2	cup vegetable oil
2	eggs or egg substitutes
1	egg white
4	cups unbleached flour
1	onion, peeled and finely chopped
1	teaspoon poppy seeds

Combine yeast and 3/4 cup warm water in a large bowl. Stir until the yeast has been distributed throughout. Let stand for several minutes. Add the sugar, salt, and oil. Beat the eggs and egg white together (save 1 tablespoon for brushing the top of the rolls) and add to the mixture. Then slowly beat in the flour. When the mixing gets tough, use your hands to knead the flour into the dough. Knead the dough for 5 minutes. Let rise for 1 hour in a covered, greased bowl. After 1 hour punch the dough down, and preheat the oven to 375°F. Taking about 1/2 cup of the dough, form a ball. Flatten slightly and place on a greased or nonstick sprayed baking sheet. The rolls will spread as they bake so leave room between them. Combine the reserved tablespoon of egg with a tablespoon of water and brush the top of each roll. Into the center of each roll press 1 tablespoon of chopped onion.

Sprinkle with some of the poppy seeds. When all the rolls have been formed, bake for 15 to 20 minutes until golden brown. Remove from the oven; let cool on a wire rack.

Per roll: 261 calories; 6 gms. protein; 35 gms. carbohydrates; 11 gms. fat; 36 mgs. cholesterol; 105 mgs. sodium

BAGELS

PAREVE • MAKES 1 DOZEN BAGELS

Making bagels is hard work, but it is fun to realize that they can be made at home. I once made them with children visiting at Thanksgiving. They woke up early, as kids will do, and I said, "Let's make bagels." So we made bagels, and they were so fascinated that they let their parents sleep.

4 to 5	cups unsifted unbleached flour
3	tablespoons sugar
1/2	teaspoon salt
1	package active dry yeast
1 1/2	cups very warm tap water (120 to 130° F)
1	egg white, beaten
1	tablespoon cold water

In a large bowl, thoroughly mix 1 1/2 cups flour, the sugar, salt, and yeast. Gradually add tap water to dry ingredients and beat 2 minutes at medium speed with an electric mixer, scraping the bowl occasionally. Add 1/2 cup flour. Beat at high speed 2 minutes, scraping the bowl occasionally. Stir in enough additional flour to make a soft dough. Turn out onto a lightly floured board and kneed until smooth and elastic, about 8 to 10 minutes. Place in an ungreased bowl. Cover and let rise in a warm place free from draft for 20 minutes. (Dough will not be doubled in bulk.) Punch down. Turn out onto a slightly floured board, and roll dough into a rectangle, 12 by 8 inches. Cut dough into 12 equal strips, 1 by 8 inches each. Pinch ends of strips together to form a circle. Place on ungreased baking sheets, cover, and let rise in a warm place, free from drafts, for 20 minutes. (Dough will not have doubled in bulk.)

Preheat oven to 375°F.

Fill a large shallow pan with water, 1¾ inches deep. Bring to a boil. Lower heat and add a few bagels at a time. Simmer 7 minutes. Remove from water and place on a towel to cool for 5 minutes. Place on ungreased baking sheets and bake for 10 minutes. Remove from oven. Brush with egg white combined with cold water, and return to oven. Bake about 20 minutes longer, or until golden brown. Remove from baking sheets and cool on wire racks.

Per bagel: 154 calories; 5 gms. protein;
33 gms. carbohydrates; 0.4 gm. fat;
0 mgs. cholesterol; 92 mgs. sodium

BOBKA

DAIRY • SERVES 16 TO 20

My grandmother Rose made a delicious bobka. During some difficult times, she took in a "boarder"—her brother Harry. When she made the bobka for him, he enjoyed it so much he would say, "a capora cake," a compliment meaning a singular cake or an outstanding cake. Long after Harry moved out, Grandma Rose's children always asked her to bake the capora cake.

I modified the recipe by using skim milk and two eggs rather than four egg yolks. And I added some chocolate chips.

DOUGH

1   *envelope active dry yeast*
¼   *cup lukewarm water*
½   *cup unsalted butter or margarine*
½   *cup sugar*
2   *eggs or egg substitutes*
1   *cup warmed skim milk*
5½ *cups unbleached flour*
¼   *teaspoon salt*
1   *tablespoon water*

FILLING

½   *teaspoon cinnamon*
1   *tablespoon sugar*
½   *cup chocolate chips*

Combine yeast and ¼ cup water in a small bowl. Allow to stand until the yeast dissolves. Cream butter and sugar in a large bowl. Beat in eggs (saving 1 tablespoon of eggs for later). Add dissolved yeast. Add milk alternately with flour and salt. Beat until batter leaves spoon and bowl. Place in

a lightly greased bowl, turning to grease top. Cover. Let rise in a warm, draft-free place for 1½ hours.

Punch down and let rise again until doubled. Preheat oven to 350°F. Lightly grease a tube pan. Roll out the dough to 12 by 10 inches. Combine cinnamon, sugar, and chocolate chips. Cover the dough with filling. Roll dough up along the 12-inch side and put into the tube pan. Combine the reserved tablespoon of egg with 1 tablespoon water. Brush top of bobka with this mixture. Let rise until double in bulk, for about one hour. Bake for 30 to 40 minutes or until top is golden brown.

Per slice (16 slices per bobka):
279 calories; 6 gms. protein;
44 gms. carbohydrates; 9 gms. fat;
43 mgs. cholesterol; 52 mgs. sodium

Per slice (20 slices per bobka):
224 calories; 5 gms. protein;
35 gms. carbohydrates; 7 gms. fat;
35 mgs. cholesterol; 41 mgs. sodium

POLENTA

PAREVE • SERVES 8 TO 10

I like polenta because it is so healthy and colorful…and really good topped with Vicki's Hot and Spicy Tomatoes and Peppers (see page 70). Polenta is a corn meal mush that can be made, poured into a pan, and refrigerated until ready to use.

5   cups cold water
1¹/₂ cups very fine white or yellow
      corn meal

In a heavy saucepan, bring the water to a boil. Turn heat to low and slowly add the corn meal, stirring constantly with a wire whisk. Continue adding and stirring until all the corn meal is added. Cover and continue cooking for 40 minutes, stirring occasionally. When the corn meal is thick and leaves the sides of the pan, remove from the heat. Pour into an oiled 9- by 9-inch baking pan. Refrigerate 3 to 4 hours or overnight until firm. Cut into squares or wedges. Place on a baking sheet and heat at 350° for 15 minutes. Place on a serving plate, and top with tomato sauce and parmesan cheese or sauce of your choice.

---

*Per serving (based on 9 servings):
70 calories; 1 gm. protein;
15 gms. carbohydrates; 0.8 gm. fat;
0 mgs. cholesterol; 1 mg. sodium*

Use fine corn meal to prepare this polenta. Top it with Vicki's Hot and Spicy Tomatoes and Peppers (see page 70).

PUMPERNICKEL BREAD

PAREVE • MAKES 2 LOAVES

Everyone should try making bread at home at least once. The smell of bread baking cannot be overestimated. This is a very hearty bread. Knead in two cups of raisins before forming the dough into loaves and you'll have raisin pumpernickel. The dough can also be made into rolls.

2   cups rye flour
1¹/₂ cups unbleached white flour
1¹/₂ cups whole wheat flour
2   cups toasted whole wheat
      bread crumbs
¹/₂ cup wheat bran
¹/₄ cup carob or cocoa powder
2   packages quick-rising yeast
¹/₂ teaspoon fennel seeds, crushed
      with a mortar and pestle
2   tablespoons caraway seeds
1   teaspoon salt
¹/₄ teaspoon ground ginger
4   tablespoons corn oil
4   tablespoons molasses or dark
      corn syrup
¹/₄ cup strong coffee or 1 tablespoon
      instant coffee dissolved in
      ¹/₄ cup water
2   cups warm water
    Cornmeal, poppy seeds, or flour

GLAZE

1   egg yolk
1   teaspoon water
1   teaspoon instant coffee

Combine the rye flour, white flour, whole wheat flour, bread crumbs, bran, carob, yeast, fennel and caraway seeds, salt, and ginger. In a large bowl, combine the oil, molasses, coffee, and warm water. Add half the dry ingredients to the liquid mixture. Beat with a wooden spoon until well combined. While continuing to mix, gradually add the rest of the dry ingredients until the dough is solid and manageable. It should be moist. Turn the dough onto a lightly floured board. Knead until smooth and firm, adding more flour to the board to keep dough from sticking. Form the dough into a ball and place in an oiled bowl. Cover the bowl with plastic wrap and a towel and let it rise in a warm, draft-free place. This should take about 30 minutes. When the dough has risen to double its size, punch it down and cut it in half. Knead each half on a lightly floured board just long enough so that it becomes firm enough to mold into a nice round shape. Sprinkle cornmeal, poppy seeds, or flour on the bottom of a baking sheet. Place the dough rounds on the sheet, and with a knife, slash a cross in the center of each round. Cover with a lightly moistened towel and let rise for ¹/₂ hour, or until double in bulk. Preheat oven to 375°F. Bake the bread for 30 minutes and then brush the tops with the glaze. Bake for 10 minutes more, then test to see if the bread is ready: It should sound hollow when the bottom is tapped. Cool on a rack.

---

*Per slice (15 slices per loaf): 98 calories;
3 gms. protein; 17 gms. carbohydrates;
2 gms. fat; 12 mgs. cholesterol;
74 mgs. sodium*

CINNAMON BUNS

DAIRY • MAKES 20 BUNS

My father's grandmother called these "tsinaming bums."

DOUGH

1   cup whole wheat flour or unbleached flour
1/4   cup sugar
1/2   teaspoon salt
1   package active dry yeast
3/4   cup skim milk
1/4   cup water
1/4   cup unsalted butter or margarine
1   egg or egg substitute
2   egg whites
2 to 3 cups unbleached flour

TOPPING AND FILLING

6   tablespoons unsalted butter or margarine
1 1/4 cups firmly packed dark brown sugar
2   teaspoons cinnamon
1/2   cup light corn syrup
1/2   cup pecan pieces
1/2   cup raisins

To prepare the dough, mix whole wheat flour, sugar, salt, and dry yeast in a large bowl. In a saucepan, heat milk, water, and butter or margarine. Add to dry ingredients and, using an electric mixer, beat at medium speed to combine, scraping bowl occasionally. Add egg, egg whites, and 1/2 cup of unbleached flour. Beat at high speed for 2 minutes. Stir in enough additional flour to make a soft dough. Knead on a lightly floured board for 8 to 10 minutes. Place in a greased bowl, turning to grease top. Cover, and let rise in a warm, draft-free place until doubled in bulk, about 1 hour.

While dough is rising, prepare topping. In a saucepan, mix 4 tablespoons of butter or margarine with 1 cup of brown sugar, 1 teaspoon of cinnamon, and the corn syrup. Cook and stir until sugar dissolves. Pour into a greased 13- by 9- by 2-inch baking pan. Sprinkle with pecan pieces.

Punch dough down and divide in half. Roll each half to a 14- by 10-inch rectangle. Melt remaining butter or margarine and brush on dough; sprinkle with remaining brown sugar, cinnamon, and raisins. Roll up to form 10-inch-long rolls. Pinch seams. Cut each roll into 10 slices. Arrange in prepared pan. Cover and let rise until doubled, about 45 minutes. Bake in a preheated oven at 375°F for 20 to 25 minutes. Cool in pan for 5 minutes, then invert onto wire rack to cool completely. Serve with sliced fruit or melon and butter or margarine on the side, if desired.

Per bun: 240 calories; 4 gms. protein; 40 gms. carbohydrates; 8 gms. fat; 11 mgs. cholesterol; 78 mgs. sodium

PITA CRISPS

PAREVE • MAKES 24 CRISPS

I like these to garnish soups, to accompany salads, or to dip into a spicy tomato sauce. They can also be rubbed with cut garlic, brushed with olive oil, spread with finely chopped onion, poppy seeds, or an herb, and baked. Add garlic, oil, tomato, and toppings after the fresh pitas are cut in half.

3   (6-inch) whole wheat pita bread rounds

Preheat oven to 400°F.

Split a pita in half to form 2 separate circles. Cut each round in quarters. Repeat with remaining 2 pitas. Place these wedges on baking sheets. Bake for 6 minutes or until crispy and browned.

Per serving (4 crisps): 53 calories; 2 gms. protein; 10 gms. carbohydrates; 0.3 gm. fat; 0 mgs. cholesterol; 108 mgs. sodium

My great grandmother made these and called them "tsinaming buns." Serve them for breakfast, with tea, or as dessert.

Rugalach

Apple Streusel Coffee Cake

Crazy Chocolate Cake

Pineapple and Raisin Compote

Passover Sponge Cake with Sliced Strawberries in White Zinfandel

Fruit and Seed Medley

Grandmom Rose's Mandel Bread

Aunt Anita's Cold Fruit Kugel

Plum Crisp

Teiglach

Honey, Almond, and Cheese Squares

Blueberries and Rice

Apple Strudel

Chocolate Swirl Cheesecake

CHAPTER VII

DESSERTS

I think of "typical" kosher dessert as compote, canned fruit, or jello with fruit in it; that's what we had in my home. For special occasions we had honey cake or sponge cake. At bar mitzvahs and weddings there was usually a chocolate bobka, rugalach, or kichel. And if we went to "the city," we always stopped for a rich and velvety strawberry or cherry cheesecake at Lindy's. Now I serve Pineapple and Raisin Compote or Fruit and Seed Medley. We should be eating more fruit for its vitamin, mineral, and fiber content, so I try to combine fruit with a cake or cookie.

Fruit is good only when it is ripe, so buy it ripe or let it ripen at home. Often fruit will become rotten rather than ripe, so watch it carefully, and refrigerate when it is ripe.

Fresh fruit is usually kosher, but some producers have been known to wax fruit with a substance containing tallow or lard, making it unkosher. Check with your grocery manager if you are uncertain.

This produce stand was owned by a cousin of Uncle Charles Hirsch in Poughkeepsie, New York. The boy on the right is Leo Hirsch, my father-in-law. The flags are in celebration of the Decoration Day parade.

RUGALACH

DAIRY • MAKES 3 DOZEN RUGALACH

Here's Cousin Rochelle Goldstein's recipe for rugalach. She says she has three or four but this one's her favorite.

¹/₂	*cup raisins*
2	*cups unbleached flour*
¹/₂	*pound butter*
8	*ounces cream cheese*
¹/₂	*teaspoon cinnamon*
¹/₂	*cup sugar*
	Raspberry preserves
	Chocolate chips (optional)
	Chopped walnuts (optional)

Plump the raisins in boiling water about 10 minutes. Drain and reserve.

Preheat oven to 350°F.

Combine flour, butter, and cream cheese. Knead until the dough becomes a workable ball. Combine the cinnamon and sugar. Roll dough out on a floured board and sprinkle with the cinnamon and sugar mixture. Cut into 2-inch squares. In the center of each square, place a pea-sized dot of preserves and/or 3 raisins (sometimes I use chocolate chips or walnuts). Roll from one corner to the opposite and shape into a crescent. Sprinkle with more cinnamon and sugar, if desired. Place on an ungreased baking sheet (they won't spread, so they can be placed fairly close to each other) and bake for 20 to 25 minutes.

Per rugalach: 99 calories; 1 gm. protein; 7 gms. carbohydrates; 7 gms. fat; 21 mgs. cholesterol; 20 mgs. sodium

APPLE STREUSEL COFFEE CAKE

DAIRY • SERVES 9

I used to make this cake in a tube pan with ½ pound butter, 3 eggs, ½ pint sour cream, and a cup of chopped nuts. Now I cut down the fat considerably by using only 4 tablespoons margarine, only 1 egg (and it could be 2 egg whites or an egg substitute), nonfat sour cream, skim milk, and ¼ the amount of the nuts. My Great-grandmother Glazier once made this apple cake and brought out the whole cake to serve a slice to her upstairs tenant, Mrs. Brown. Great-grandmom's English was limited, so she said, "Take, Mrs. Brown," and Mrs. Brown picked up the whole cake and went back to her apartment. My grandmother and her brothers and sisters came home and demanded an explanation from their mother as to what had happened to the cake!

1¾	*cups unbleached flour*
1	*teaspoon baking powder*
4	*tablespoons margarine*
½	*cup sugar*
1	*egg or egg substitute*
1	*teaspoon vanilla*
½	*cup skim milk*
½	*cup nonfat sour cream*
1	*Red Delicious apple, peeled and thinly sliced*

TOPPING

3	*tablespoons brown sugar*
2	*teaspoons flour*
1	*teaspoon cinnamon*
¼	*cup chopped walnuts*

Preheat oven to 350°F.

Sift the flour and baking powder into a small bowl. In another bowl, cream the margarine and sugar until light and fluffy. Add the egg and beat well. Add the vanilla. Then add to milk and sour cream alternately with the flour mixture. Spoon the batter into a 9- by 9-inch nonstick, sprayed or Teflon pan. Smooth out the batter. Layer the sliced apples in rows on top.

To prepare the topping, combine all ingredients and spoon over the apples. Bake for 20 to 25 minutes until the topping is golden brown and the apples are tender.

Per serving: 229 calories; 5 gms. protein; 34 gms. carbohydrates; 8 gms. fat; 24 mgs. cholesterol; 62 mgs. sodium

*U*ncle Mickey loves chocolate
cake and Aunt Eleanor loves
making it for him.

CRAZY CHOCOLATE CAKE

PAREVE • SERVES 9

This recipe was given to me by my Aunt Eleanor, who prepares this cholesterol-free cake for my Uncle Mickey. It was one of the recipes given out in a rehab program for heart patients. It is a very light, low-fat, delicious cake. Aunt Eleanor adds icing, but I top it with jam.

³/₄ *cup unbleached flour*
¹/₂ *cup sugar*
3 *tablespoons cocoa powder*
¹/₂ *teaspoon baking soda*
1¹/₂ *teaspoons vinegar*
¹/₂ *teaspoon vanilla*
3 *tablespoons canola oil*
¹/₂ *cup hot water*
3 *tablespoons seedless raspberry jam*

Preheat oven to 350°F.

Sift all dry ingredients into an ungreased 8- by 8-inch pan. Make three holes in the dry ingredients. Pour vinegar into the first hole, vanilla into the second hole, and oil into the third hole. Pour the hot water over all and stir with a wooden spoon until completely mixed. Bake in the preheated oven for 10 minutes or until a toothpick inserted in the center of the cake comes out clean. Heat the jam in a saucepan or microwave oven and brush over the top to glaze.

*Per serving: 144 calories; 2 gms. protein;
24 gms. carbohydrates; 5 gms. fat;
0 mgs. cholesterol; 47 mgs. sodium*

PINEAPPLE AND RAISIN COMPOTE

PAREVE • SERVES 6

This compote is especially good for pineapple that is too hard or underripe to eat raw.

¹/₂ *fresh pineapple, cut vertically*
2 *tablespoons water*
2 *tablespoons raisins*
2 *tablespoons packed brown sugar*

Peel and remove hard core from pineapple. Cut into 10 to 12 thin slices. In a microwave-safe dish with a cover, overlap the pineapple slices. Sprinkle the water, raisins, and sugar over the pineapple. Cover and microwave on high for 2 minutes, then let stand for 5 minutes. Serve at room temperature.

To prepare the pineapple on top of the stove, add pineapple, ¹/₄ cup water, raisins, and brown sugar to a pot. Bring to a boil, cover, and boil for 5 minutes. Remove from heat. Overlap pineapple slices on a flat serving dish and pour raisins and syrup over the pineapple.

*Per serving: 65 calories; 4 gms. protein;
16 gms. carbohydrates; 0.3 gm. fat;
0 mgs. cholesterol; 2 mgs. sodium*

*This Crazy Chocolate Cake is delicious. No
one will ever guess how low in fat and
cholesterol it really is.*

FRUIT AND SEED MEDLEY

PAREVE • SERVES 6

1 (16-ounce) can peach slices packed
     in juice
1 apple, cored and coarsely chopped
1 banana, sliced
6 strawberries, hulled and sliced
1/4 cup currants
2 tablespoons sunflower seeds
    Kiwi slices (for garnish)
    Starfruit slices (for garnish)
    Mint leaves (for garnish)

Combine the fruits and seeds in a serving bowl. Garnish with kiwi, starfruit, and mint.

---

*Per serving: 91 calories; 2 gms. protein;
19 gms. carbohydrates; 2 gms. fat;
0 mgs. cholesterol; 4 mgs. sodium*

GRANDMOM ROSE'S MANDEL BREAD

PAREVE • MAKES 3 DOZEN

After Grandmom made these and they had cooled, she put the pieces in a bowl and covered them with a clean dish towel. She kept this bowl on the dresser in her bedroom because if the mandel bread was left in the kitchen, it would all be eaten by the end of the day.

Grandmom Rose's Mandel Bread was, and still is, a family favorite.

3 eggs or egg substitutes
1 cup sugar
1/2 cup vegetable oil
3 teaspoons vanilla
3 1/4 cups unbleached flour
2 teaspoons baking powder
1/4 cup chopped walnuts
2 tablespoons cocoa powder
    Sugar

Preheat oven to 325°F.

In a medium bowl, beat eggs. Add sugar and mix well. Add oil and vanilla. In a separate bowl, combine flour, baking powder, and chopped walnuts. Add to the egg mixture and stir until well blended. Divide the dough in half and add cocoa to half the dough.

Take 1/2 of the vanilla half and 1/2 of the chocolate half, and squeeze them together to form a long marble roll about 13 inches long by 3 inches wide. This is easily done right on a baking sheet with floured hands. Repeat the process, forming one more marble roll with the remaining dough. Sprinkle sugar on top. Bake these rolls for 30 minutes. Remove the pan from the oven and cut into 3/4 inch slices. Cool.

---

*Per piece: 102 calories; 2 gms. protein;
14 gms. carbohydrates; 4 gms. fat;
18 mgs. cholesterol; 24 mgs. sodium*

Grandmom Rose loved to make mandel bread for the "kinderlach."

HONEY, ALMOND, AND CHEESE SQUARES

DAIRY; PAREVE WITHOUT
TOPPING • MAKES ONE 9- BY 9-INCH
CAKE, CUT INTO 25 SQUARES

Honey cake is traditionally served with tea; the honey and almond suggests it comes from the Middle East.

I modified this recipe by cutting down on the amount of eggs and oil. It is delicious with or without the topping and is pareve if prepared without the topping.

2	cups unbleached flour
1	teaspoon baking powder
1/4	teaspoon baking soda
1/2	teaspoon cinnamon
1/4	teaspoon ground cloves
1	egg or egg substitute
1	egg white
1/4	cup sugar
1/2	cup honey
2	tablespoons vegetable oil
1/2	cup strong cold coffee

TOPPING

1	pound skim milk ricotta cheese
6	tablespoons sugar
1	egg white
2	ounces slivered almonds

Preheat oven to 350°F.

Combine the flour, baking powder, baking soda, cinnamon, and cloves in a bowl. In another bowl, beat the egg and egg white with an electric mixer until foamy. Add the sugar and honey and continue beating. Beat in the oil. Add about half of the cold coffee and mix well. Add the dry ingredients and the remaining coffee. Pour the batter into a lightly greased or nonstick sprayed 9- by 9-inch pan.

To prepare the topping, beat together the ricotta cheese, sugar, and egg white and slowly pour over the cake batter. Top with the slivered almonds. Bake for 45 minutes. Let the cake cool before cutting.

Per serving (with cheese topping):
128 calories; 4 gms. protein;
19 gms. carbohydrates; 4 gms. fat;
14 mgs. cholesterol; 52 mgs. sodium

Per serving (without cheese topping):
78 calories; 1 gm. protein;
15 gms. carbohydrates; 1 gm. fat;
9 mgs. cholesterol; 27 mgs. sodium

BLUEBERRIES AND RICE

PAREVE • SERVES 6

Rice pudding is a favorite dessert but it usually contains a lot of eggs and cream or milk. This rice dessert is pareve, contains no eggs, and is high in dietary fiber. I like basmati rice but brown or any other rice is good. My husband loves old-fashioned rice pudding and he thinks this version is delicious.

2	cups cooked basmati or brown rice, or any rice of your choice
2	cups fresh blueberries or thawed and drained frozen blueberries
3	tablespoons firmly packed brown sugar
2	tablespoons wheat bran
2	tablespoons whole wheat flour
2	tablespoons chopped almonds
1/2	teaspoon ground cinnamon
2	tablespoons pareve margarine

Preheat oven to 375°F.

Combine cooked rice, blueberries, and 2 tablespoons brown sugar. Coat 6 individual custard cups or a 1½-quart baking dish with nonstick spray. Place the rice mixture in the cups or baking dish; set aside. Combine the bran, flour, almonds, the remaining tablespoon of brown sugar, and the cinnamon in a bowl. Cut in margarine until mixture resembles coarse meal. Sprinkle evenly over rice mixture. Bake for 15 to 20 minutes or until thoroughly heated. Serve warm, garnished with additional fresh blueberries.

To prepare in a microwave, cook 1½-quart dish uncovered on high 4 to 5 minutes. Individual dishes can be microwaved for 2 minutes. Let stand 2 minutes before serving.

Per serving: 188 calories; 3 gms. protein;
32 gms. carbohydrates; 6 gms. fat;
0 mgs. cholesterol; 49 mgs. sodium

Blueberries and Rice is a more healthy
version of traditional rice pudding.

*U*ncle Abe and Aunt Jeanette
in front of their apartment.
When we visited them, we were
treated to a subway ride; when
they came to visit us, we were
treated to Apple Strudel.

APPLE STRUDEL

PAREVE WITH PAREVE MARGARINE; DAIRY
WITH BUTTER • SERVES 12

Aunt Jeanette Turim occasionally came to visit us from the Bronx. When she visited, we had strudel. She spent the day making the dough, pressing and stretching it over a clean cloth on the card table. When the card table was covered with dough, it was spread with apples, raisins, and nuts, formed into long rolls and baked. Everyone looked forward to a visit from Aunt Jeanette.

This recipe uses commercial phyllo dough; most brands are kosher. The filling tastes just the way I remember Aunt Jeanette's.

FILLING

2¹/₂   apples, unpeeled and shredded
¹/₂   cup golden raisins
¹/₄   cup sliced or chopped almonds
2   tablespoons fine bread crumbs
2   tablespoons honey
¹/₂   teaspoon cinnamon

DOUGH

9   phyllo sheets
2   tablespoons vegetable oil
2   tablespoons pareve margarine or
    butter, melted
2   teaspoons honey

Preheat oven to 350°F.

Combine all filling ingredients in a bowl and set aside.

To prepare phyllo sheets, follow package directions. If frozen, phyllo should be thawed in the refrigerator. Remove the phyllo from packaging material only when ready to prepare strudel.

Combine oil and melted margarine or butter in a small dish. Lay out 3 phyllo sheets, one on top of the other, on a piece of plastic wrap. Brush the top sheet with the oil-margarine mixture. Near one edge of the shorter side, spoon out a row of the apple filling. Using plastic wrap, roll the phyllo over the filling, continuing to roll to the other end. Place this roll on a nonstick, sprayed baking sheet. Do the same with the remaining sheets of phyllo, making three rolls.

Add the honey to the remaining oil-margarine mix. Brush this on top of the three strudel rolls on the baking sheet. Use all the mixture. These rolls can be frozen at this point and baked later.

Bake for 30 minutes or until browned. Cool slightly and cut each roll into 4 slices.

Per serving: 153 calories; 3 gms. protein;
25 gms. carbohydrates; 6 gms. fat;
0 mgs. cholesterol; 68 mgs. sodium

CHOCOLATE SWIRL CHEESECAKE

DAIRY • SERVES 16

This book had to include a cheesecake. When I think cheesecake, I think of glazed strawberries on a rich and creamy cheesecake like the ones served at Lindy's, Juniors, or Wolfies. When I bake those cheesecakes with all the butter, eggs, cream cheese, and sour cream, I think I am killing my guests....I can watch their cholesterol rise. So I don't bake them anymore.

1/4	cup chocolate cookie crumbs
24	ounces 1 percent low-fat or nonfat cottage cheese
16	ounces light cream cheese
1	cup plus 2 tablespoons sugar
2	eggs or egg substitutes
1	teaspoon vanilla
3	tablespoons unsweetened cocoa
4	egg whites
1/4	teaspoon cream of tartar

Prehat oven to 325°F.

Coat the bottom of a 10-inch springform pan with nonstick spray. Sprinkle with chocolate cookie crumbs and set aside.

In a food processor fitted with the metal blade, process cottage cheese and cream cheese until smooth. Add 1 cup of the sugar, the eggs, and vanilla. Process until smooth. Pour into a medium bowl. Remove 1/4 of the batter to a small bowl, add the cocoa, and mix until smooth.

Beat egg whites and cream of tartar at high speed until foamy. Gradually add remaining 2 tablespoons sugar, one table-spoon at a time, beating until stiff peaks form. Fold 1/4 of the egg-white mixture into the cocoa mixture. Fold remaining egg-white mixture into the plain cheese mixture.

Spoon alternating mounds of cocoa-cheese mixture and plain cheese mixture into the prepared pan; swirl with a knife to create a marbled effect. Bake for 50 minutes or until almost set. Remove from the oven and cool 15 minutes. Cover and chill at least 8 hours.

Per serving: 217 calories;
11 gms. protein; 23 gms. carbohydrates;
9 gms. fat; 52 mgs. cholesterol;
292 mgs. sodium

APPENDICES

KOSHER SYMBOLS

Certain registered symbols appear on commercially packaged products to designate the product is kosher: simply finding a K on a product does not mean a processed food has been examined by a rabbinical authority. It is legally possible for a manufacturer to have no rabbinical supervision and still use a K to designate its claim that the product is kosher.

Pareve, or parve, is a term used on labels to designate that a product contains neither meat, milk, nor their by-products. The U.S. Government and the Jewish Code may differ on this designation. For example, sodium caseinate by Jewish code is a dairy or milk by-product, but is found in foods labeled "non-dairy," such as non-dairy creamer. You should read product ingredient labels to make sure a dairy product is not used in a meat or pareve meal. (Labels marked pareve are sought by those with milk allergies.)

In each locality, a rabbi or kashruth organization must inspect the food manufacturer's facility should they wish its product to be labeled kosher. Each rabbi or organization has a symbol that the manufacturer or processor can use to show that the ingredient and the production of the food is kosher; symbols are often used because they require less label space than the term "prepared under strict orthodox supervision."

The symbols that follow are both commonly found and reliable. You can check the reliability of symbols not included here by contacting a rabbi.

PAREVE or PARVE

Contains no milk or meat products or by-products

The OU: Union of Orthodox Jewish Congregations, 45 West 36th Street, New York, NY 10018

KAJ

The KAJ: Beth Din of K'hal Adath Jeshurun, 85–93 Bennett Avenue, New York, NY 10033

The Star K: Star-K Kosher Certification, 7504 Seven Mile Lane, Baltimore, MD 21208

The Heart K: Igud Hakashrus of Los Angeles, 415 North Spaulding, Los Angeles, CA 90036

The OV: Kashruth Inspection Service of the Vaad Hoeir of Saint Louis, 4 Millstone Campus, St. Louis, MO 63146

Wholesome and Kosher: Rabbi Yehuda Kelemer, Young Israel of West Hempstead, 630 Hempstead Avenue, West Hempstead, NY 11552

Upper Midwest Kashruth: Rabbi Asher Zeilingold, 1001 Prior Avenue South, St. Paul, MN 55116

The OK: The Organized Kashrus Laboratories, 1372 Carroll Street, Brooklyn, NY 11213

The KOF-K: KOF-K Kosher Supervision, 1444 Queen Anne Road, Teaneck, NJ 07666

National Kashruth, 1 Route 306, Monsey, NY 10952

KOSHER WINES

The CRC: Chicago Rabbinical Council, 3525 West Peterson Avenue, Suite 415, Chicago, IL 60659

The VH or the KVH: Vaad Harabonim (Vaad Hakashrus) of Massachusetts, 177 Tremont Street, Boston, MA 02111

The Parallelogram K: Rabbi Dr. Bernard Poupko, 5715 Beacon Street, Pittsburgh, PA 15217

Diamond K: Rabbi Zevulun Glixman, 1425 South West 85th Avenue, Miami, FL 33144; or Orthodox Vaad of Philadelphia, 717 Callowhill Street, Philadelphia, PA 19123

The Texas K: Texas K Kosher Supervision, 5807 Harvest Hill Road, Dallas, TX 75230

Over the last decade there has been an explosion in the variety and quality of kosher wines.

There are wonderful reds and whites coming from new or revivified vineyards in California, New York, France, Italy, and Israel.

From French champagnes to chablis, from California chardonnays to Israeli cabernet sauvignons, there are kosher wines for every taste and every food. I have listed a few of the best, but check out your local store—the owner may have something special.

CHAMPAGNE AND SPARKLING WINES

Comte de Crissier, Brut Epernay NV
Carmel Brut Reserve Cuvee (Israel)

EUROPEAN WHITE WINES

Chateau Chateauneuf semi-dry Bordeaux
Chablis Domaine La Roche, 1987
Sancerre, Alphonse Mellot, 1988
Chateau de la Grave Dry Bordeaux
(Kedem)
Leone Pinot Grigio, 1988 (Italy)

EUROPEAN RED WINES

Barons de Rothschild, Haut-Medoc, 1987
Chateau Labegorce, Margaux, 1987
Chateau du Grava, 1988, Bordeaux
Superieur

Beaujolais, Louis Tete, 1989
Chateau la Reze Minervois, 1989

ISRAELI WINES

Yarden Vineyards (Golan Heights)
Yarden Sauvignon Blanc, 1989
Yarden Chardonnay, 1988 (limited)
Yarden Cabernet Sauvignon, 1986/7
Yarden Merlot, 1988 (limited, inquire)
Yarden White Riesling, 1990 (limited)
Yarden Cabernet Blanc, 1990 (Blush
Wine)
Yarden Mount Hermon White, 1989
Yarden Mount Hermon Red, 1990
Yarden Rose of Cabernet, 1989/90
Yarden Port Blanc, 1989 (limited)

GOLAN VINEYARDS (GOLAN HEIGHTS, YARDEN WINERY)

Golan Cabernet Sauvignon, 1986
Golan Nouveau Galil Red, 1988/89
Golan Sauvignon Blanc, 1988/89
Golan Emerald Riesling, 1988
Golan Demi-sec, 1988
Golan Muscat, 1988
Golan Rose of Cabernet, 1989

GAMLA VINEYARDS (GOLAN HEIGHTS, YARDEN WINERY)

Sauvignon Blanc Special Reserve, 1988
Sauvignon Blanc, 1988
Chardonnay, 1987/88

Cabernet Sauvignon Special Reserve, 1986
Cabernet Sauvignon, 1987
Cabernet Blanc, 1990 (blush wine)
Emerald Hill White, 1988
Semi-Dry White, 1988
Semi-Dry Red (Rose of Cabernet), 1990
Muscato de Gamla, 1989
Sauvignon Blanc Botrytis Late Harvest

AMERICAN WINES

WEINSTOCK VINEYARDS

(First kosher Sonoma Valley Vineyard)
Chardonnay, 1989/90
White Zinfandel, Blush Wine, 1990

GAN EDEN WINERY, CALIFORNIA

Cabernet Sauvignon, 1987
Chardonnay, 1988
Fume Blanc (Sauvignon Blanc), 1988

HAGAFEN WINERY, CALIFORNIA

Pinot Noir Blanc

KEDEM CALIFORNIA SELECTION BARON JAQUAB DE HERZOG

Chardonnay, 1989
Cabernet Sauvignon, 1989
White Zinfandel, Blush Wine, 1989
Sauvignon Blanc, 1989

For those who want the traditional sweet wines, I suggest:

Kedem Concord
Kedem Malaga

INDEX